W9-CFU-700

POLAND

Dear Stach,

Thank you very much
for all you had done
to my family. Love Elisab

CHRISTIAN PARMA

Text WOJCIECH GIEŁŻYŃSKI

POLAND

Wydawnictwo PARMA® PRESS

Wasilków near Białystok. Flat land dominates in the Polish landscape, often featuring a cross.

Cover photos: Mazovian landscape;
          Chopin Monument in Warsaw Łazienki Park
Title pages: Sunset on Lake Tuchomskie

Photos: CHRISTIAN PARMA
Text: WOJCIECH GIEŁŻYŃSKI

Layout: BOGNA PARMA
Map: MARIUSZ SZELEREWICZ
Translation: ELŻBIETA KOWALEWSKA

Photocomposition: Studio PARMA IMAGE +48 22 / 675 08 87

Printed by: HELIOS EXPRINT, Červený Kostelec, Czech Republic

Publisher: PARMA PRESS, 03-310 Warszawa, Staniewicka 12,
+48 22 / 675 87 50, 675 80 07, 614 30 44

3rd edition

ISBN 83-85743-28-6

© Copyright by Wydawnictwo PARMA® PRESS, Warszawa 1999

*Bronze statues
of the Polish
Piasts Mieszko I
and Bolesław the
Brave in the
Golden Chapel of
Poznań Cathedral*

INTRODUCTION

The Poles: History and a Touch of the Present

Poland entered Europe during a tense period. The year 1000 was soon to come. As always happens at the close of any millennium, people were scared to death of the approaching doomsday.

In King Lothar's France the great Carolingian dynasty was already nearing its end. England had its King Edgar of Wessex, too peaceful for his stormy time, since the island was repeatedly invaded and plundered by Norman troops from Scandinavia. Having crushed the harassing bands of Magyars, Germany was growing in power under Otto I, called the Great, a sort of Chancellor Helmut Kohl of that time. Otto I was also driven by an ambition to unite not only Germany, but the whole of Europe and the whole of the Christian world. He had just then been crowned emperor.

The 10th-century Poles absolutely liked it! They were just emerging out of the tribal magma and had to split up with paganism as quickly as they now wish to forget communism. In order to avoid being converted to Christianity by sword and to enter the forerunner of the European Union, they needed a protector.

Otto I was quite inclined to be such a protector. He wanted to defend himself from the savage East, constantly threatening Germany with hordes of Huns, Vandals, Avars and the like. So the Emperor gave his assent to the marriage of his vassal Duke of Bohemia, Boleslav the Cruel's beloved daughter Dobravka with Mieszko, some little known duke of the Polane tribe. The duke was growing in strength and it was the Polanes who began the formation of the Polish state by forcing other West Slavonic tribes to unite.

Historians are still fascinated by the question of whether the young couple had consummated their marriage before they were properly wed. Most of them favour the shameful opinion that Duchess Dobravka had shared her bed with a pagan for at least one full year before her husband was solemnly baptized. The ceremony took place most probably in Ratisbon (now Regensburg), in the year 966.

Such was Poland's way of becoming a part of Europe a thousand years ago, when the first attempt at continental integration was being made. It surely was a successful entrance, for within two years following the baptism the Polish neophytes were sent a bishop of their own, named Jordan. Even the Bohemians, Christians already for more than a century, were granted such privilege only five years after the Poles. It would seem quite possible that the western countries were more interested in a large Poland than in a tiny Bohemia. Maybe they saw Poland as a promising trade partner. The famous Arab traveller Ibrahim-ibn-Yaqub of Tortosa, well informed at Otto I's court, wrote that the land of Mieszko, the largest of all Slavonic dukedoms, abounded in food, especially meat and honey, and its ruler owned a strong army of three thousand warriors.

Today Poles yearn to hear Western journalists similarly praise the values of their country, aspiring to join NATO and the European Union.

Poland has been so unfortunate in its history that it has to strive anew for its admission to the European structures. Not all Westerners are in favour of that. As in the times of Mieszko Poland could not rid itself of the label of a postpagan country, so today, despite the popularity gained by Lech Wałęsa, it continues to be referred to as a postcommunist state.

The Poles' Coming of Age

Luckily, other opinions prevail in the West. Poland is ever more frequently described as a 'European tiger' – which sounds least convincing to the Poles themselves. Poland is far from being as wealthy as the present European Union members. Unemployment and inflation are still very high. However, in recent years the economic growth rate has been truly record-breaking. The poverty margins are shrinking. Rich and very rich people grow in number. They can easily afford a holiday on the Seychelles, skiing at Chamonix or even a mansion of their own in imitation of a castle. Shops have already met Western standards. Cities and towns resemble those in Germany or France, not necessarily in tidiness but surely in the amount of adverts for the same products as in the West. Every now and then you see a newly-built house, skyscraper or church, as well as new restaurants, bars and pubs.

In short, Poland is quickly becoming more and more like the countries it may within a few years accompany in the European and Atlantic communities. At the same time, many parts of Poland have maintained their traditional ways, old-fashioned charm and naturalness, to the satisfaction of Poles as well as foreign, especially Western visitors. The latter are attracted by the somewhat east-

*Sections
of the Białowieża
Forest are an
attraction for
many foreign
visitors*

ern exotic character of this country.

Poland looks Eastern to the West and Western to the East not only because it lies exactly in the geographical centre of Europe, i.e. at equal distances from Portugal and the Ural Mountains as well as from the Greek Peloponnesus and the North Cape in Norway. There are also cultural reasons: the great European borderline between the Roman and Byzantine traditions, today as distinct as ever, runs slight west of Poland's eastern frontier. Since the dawn of history Poland combined its fate with Western civilization, at the same time constantly maintaining vivid relations with the East. From there came, for instance, some old Polish trends in fashion and interior design. We can thus agree on a compromise that Poland, along with the Czech Republic, Hungary and Austria, belongs to Central Europe. This idea is extremely popular in all these countries, which had for a long time remained within the sphere of influence of the Habsburg court.

Poland is characterized by having completely disappeared every now an then from the map for a long time. Poland's geographical contredance - the shuffle of its territory first far eastwards and then back westwards - resulted from the expansionist tendencies of its powerful neighbours. It was never easy to stand up to them, as only Poland's north and south borders, the sea and the mountains, are naturally strong. Other borders, unprotected by nature, were easily crossed. Therefore Polish territories were often seized by warlike peoples starting from the early Middle Ages.

The Poles' Stormy Youth

Let us go back for a short while to the beginnings of the Polish state. King Mieszko I and Dobravka had a son named Bolesław. This energetic ruler, named the Brave, managed to withstand the German pressure. At times he even kept normal and friendly relations with the Holy Roman Empire. He obtained the crown, a symbol of sovereignty, towards the end of his life in 1205. Under Bolesław the Brave Poland quickly grew into a big state, with more or less the same territory is has now. For a short time it also controlled Bohemia and Moravia. Gniezno and Poznań were the successive Polish capitals.

Alas, the 11th-century prosperity and security of Poland turned out to be short-lived. In the following century the country was divided into several independent duchies, which was quite a common procedure in feudal Europe. These duchies were further subdivided. Some of them, like those of Silesia and Pomerania, drifted away from their ancient Polish roots towards Germany and

Bohemia to finally come under their rule.

In those difficult times the Mongol invasion befell Poland. At the battle of Legnica (Liegnitz) in 1241 Batu Khan's horde completely defeated the Polish knights. However, themselves decimated, the Mongols were unable to advance further west, their ultimate goal. Europe could relax and Poland's role as a bulwark of Christendom was fulfilled well for the first time. It gained this country some popularity in the West, where the Mongols were feared like fiends; they terrified the West as much as the communists did seven hundred years later.

Poland was united again in the 14th century by a modest duke of the small principality of Cujavia, Władysław the Short. He drove off various foreign rulers and left a consolidated state to his son Casimir the Great, the last Polish sovereign of the Piast dynasty. Casimir put the country and its economy to order and developed trade. He is said to have found Poland built of wood and left it built of stone. He also founded a university in Cracow, thus linking the fledgling Polish culture with the West.

But Poland lost the provinces on the River Oder to Brandenburg (later Prussia), while the Teutonic Order, spreading like a tumour over Polish, Baltic Prussian and Lithua-nian land, captured the Vistula delta. Such losses could hardly be compensated for by some territorial gains in the east.

The Teutonic Knights went on expanding. They completely cut Poland off from the Baltic Sea and threatened the very existence of Lithuania. Both countries were saved by Queen Jadviga from the Hungarian branch of the Angevins. For the sake of her new homeland, she broke the engagement with Wilhelm of Habsburg and married a pagan, Grand Duke of Lithuania Władysław Jagiełło, resulting in the conversion of the Lithuanians to Christianity and their alliance (and later a union) with the Poles. The united forces of both nations defeated the Teutonic Knights near Grunwald in 1410, at one of the greatest battles of the late Middle Ages. Although the Teutonic Order continued to act for another half-century, it no longer posed a deadly threat to its neighbours. Poland entered its Golden Age. In the 16th century it became a great power, the largest and one of the richest countries of Europe.

Cracow developed into one of the most renowned cities of Europe, largely because of the excellent Cracow Academy, which still exists today. Poland became a haven for heretics, Jews and all sorts of dissidents coming from the West, for despite the domination of Roman Catholicism there were neither persecutions nor religious wars in Poland, as happened in other parts of Europe. In the mid-16th century the last Jagiellon, King Sigismund Augustus, voiced a statement to his subjects that none of his contemporary monarchs would dare to pronounce: 'I am not the king of your conscience'.

Following the end of the Jagiellonian dynasty, a system of electing kings by the nobility was introduced. The vast numbers of Polish noblemen, endowed with many rights and privileges, preferred to choose foreign kings from famous European families. It fostered the development of foreign relations, but it was certainly bad for the administration of the state. Poland's system at that early time already resembled later republic states, in which monarchs were replaced by presidents with limited powers. The role of the *Sejm*, the Polish parliament of the nobility, grew steadily. Its state-killing rule of *liberum veto* allowed any individual deputy to cease the debate and paralyse the governing process.

The 17th century was therefore far less prosperous for Poland, a country with weak governance and a growing number of conflicts. To the east the Grand Duchy of Muscovy, the precursor of Russia, was rapidly

Gniezno Cathedral, the coronation place of five Polish kings

expanding. The Ukraine, then under Polish rule, underwent a great Cossack rebellion. The Swedish invaded Poland from the north and for several years occupied the whole country along with its new capital, Warsaw. They only could not seize the Jasna Góra fortified monastery at Częstochowa, the sanctuary of the Holy Virgin Mary. This made Her the main object of cult in Polish Roman Catholic rite. Until this day millions of Poles keep going on pilgrimages to Jasna Góra, which is known as 'the Polish Lourdes'.

In addition to that, Poland was raided by the Turkish and Tartar armies – now winning, now being defeated. The last great triumph over the Turks was achieved by the famous Polish heavy cavalry – the hussars – led by King John III Sobieski in the crucial battle of Vienna in 1683. By saving Vienna, Poland acted as a liberator of Europe and a bulwark of Christianity for the second time.

The Fall and Revival of the Poles

The 18th century was disastrous for Poland. Under the weak rule of the Saxon dynasty the central authority dwindled and the internal affairs were in a complete mess. The 'noble democracy' turned into anarchy and each aristocratic family carried out its own egocentric policy. The Russian, Swedish and Prussian armies roamed freely over Polish land. It was not until the end of the century that the Poles seemed to wake up and made some attempts to reform education, the army and the economy. The crowning achievement was the 3rd May Constitution of 1791, being very progressive for that time. The world's second - after the American - and Europe's first constitutional act, it was aimed at steering the country out of chaos and modernizing its system.

But the national spurt came too late. After three partitions - in 1772, 1792 and 1795 - Poland, torn apart by Russia, Prussia and Austria, disappeared from the map. Some hope emerged during the time of Napoleon Bonaparte. The Poles formed an army of more than a hundred thousand soldiers and fought at his side till the battle of Leipzig, known as the Battle of Nations. Three quarters of the Polish soldiers were killed or taken prisoner. The fate of Poland was sealed at the Congress of Vienna in 1815. No such country was to exist for a hundred years to follow.

Very soon the Poles rose to fight for their independence. The first rising took place in response to the Second Partition of 1792. It was led by Tadeusz Kościuszko, a hero of two nations, as he had earlier fought for the independence of the United States. The next and greatest Polish armed uprising in November 1830 saved... Belgium, for it stopped the tsar-

Such monumental Gothic structures as the castle and cathedral at Kwidzyń are traces of the Teutonic Order's presence in Poland

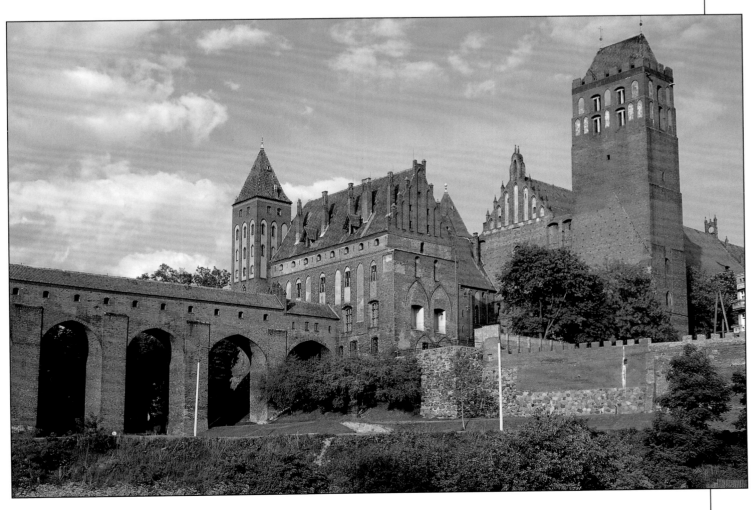

The Golden Age in Poland was marked by the activity of the Cracow Academy. The Collegium Maius of the present Jagiellonian University

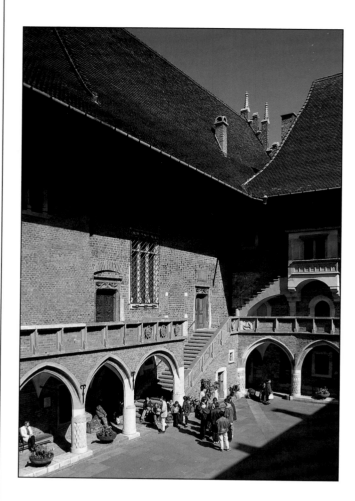

Fortified Jasna Góra Monastery, which resisted the Swedish invasion in the 17th c.

ist army from proceeding to suppress the rebellion in that country. When the Russians seized Warsaw in 1831, the French minister Sebastiani made his famous, or rather infamous statement: 'L'ordre regne à Varsovie'.

Not always the West was so cynical about Poland, though. Thousands of Polish insurgents found their refuge on the banks of the Seine, Thames, Moselle, Rhine and Tiber. When another insurrection broke out in January 1863, a few hundred Western volunteers joined the Polish units. But this rising also ended in failure. Numerous Poles were hanged, thousands of them were sent into exile to Siberia. Thus, the future Great War of Nations, a dream envisaged by the national bard Adam Mickiewicz, remained the only solution.

From the Poles' point of view, the war of 1914-18 ended in a miracle. All three partitioning powers were defeated and disintegrated. The dreams of generations came true: the Polish state was revived. Its first head of state was Józef Piłsudski. He started his fight for independence in the underground Polish Socialist Party. During the First World War he commanded the Legions formed within the Austro-Hungarian army. However, after driving the Russians out of central Poland, Piłsudski let dissolve the Legions he had formed so laboriously, for he intended to shift his political ground. Towards the end of the

war he took the side of the Western Allies, already supported by other Polish military formations in France.

The attitude of the United States President Woodrow Wilson played an important role in the rebirth of Poland. In his presidential address in January 1917 he declared that Poland should be united and independent. It became reality on 11 November 1918.

However, Poland was soon bound to face another dramatic trial: the Bolshevik invasion in 1920. In the battle of Warsaw the young Polish Army managed to repel the units of General Tukhachevsky, who had been planning to conquer Germany and the rest of Europe. He did not even cross the Vistula. For the third time in history Poland acted as a bulwark.

After a century and a half of slavery, Poland was coming back to life with difficulty, but the Poles enjoyed their 'regained mess', as it was described by the writer Juliusz Kaden-Bandrowski. The first years of integration and reconstruction of the country were auspicious. The Poles are known for their powers of improvisation. Unfortunately, persistence is not their main virtue. Poland was

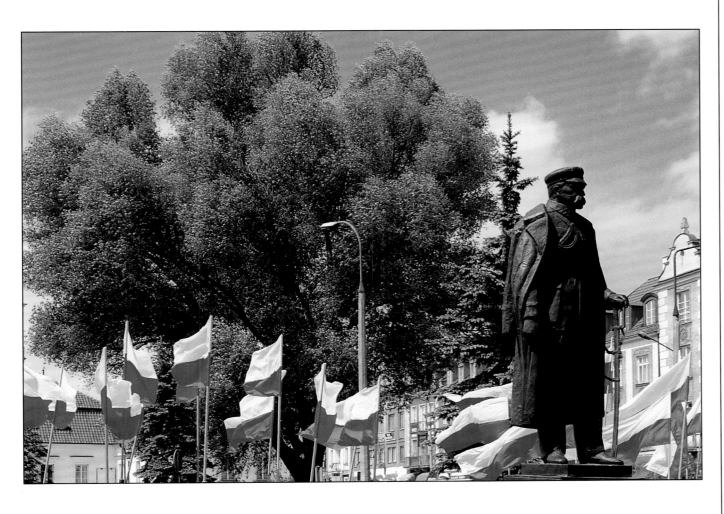

Józef Piłsudski became the head of the revived Polish state. One of numerous statues dedicated to him - in Białystok

plagued by political disputes, government crises, workers' protests and peasant riots. In 1926 Marshal Piłsudski staged a military coup, which earned him a very unfavourable opinion in the West. This opinion, still adhered to sometimes, is not quite fair. His authoritarian rule never resembled fascism, which already controlled Italy and was soon to infect Germany, Portugal, Spain and other countries. Although personally Piłsudski hated 'Sejmocracy', the parliamentary system was maintained in Poland. It is quite possible that his coup saved the country from totalitarianism, towards which the extreme right wing had been heading.

Down again

Twenty years of independence healed Poland. The integration of the former partition zones was unexpectedly quick. Modern industrial works and the large port of Gdynia were built. Poland formed a strong army and was the first state to resist Hitler's aggression. His attack on Poland on 1 September 1939 unleashed the Second World War. Invaded by Stalin from the other side, Poland was soon overwhelmed, but its soldiers would never stop fighting. Some Polish divisions took part in the defence of France. Polish soldiers fought at Narvik in Norway and defended Tobruk in Libya. They achieved great success in the Italian campaign by capturing the major Ger-

man bastion at Monte Cassino. Polish aircraft pilots fought magnificently in the Battle of Britain. On many seas marines fought under the white and red flag. Polish armoured units took part in the liberation of France, Belgium and Holland. Polish divisions set up within the Red Army finally came as far as Berlin. In occupied Poland the struggle was carried on by underground forces and forest partisans of the Home Army, formed by the London government in exile. Two insurrections broke out in the capital: the rising at the Jewish

Monument of the Jewish Ghetto Uprising in Warsaw

Oświęcim-
Auschwitz
is a symbol of the
Holocaust. The
cremating
furnaces are
a frightening
document of
Nazi genocide

Lech Wałęsa,
the leader of
fighting Solidar-
ity, then the
President of free
Poland

The birth of
Solidarity
initiated the new
Springtime of
Nations in
Europe

decided upon by the superpowers at the conferences in Yalta and Potsdam. Washington and London pretended to believe in Uncle Joseph's good intentions (it is hardly probable that they really did) and they actually left Poland under his control. Poland lost more eastern territories to the Soviet Union than it gained as compensation from Germany in the west. Anyway, the land given to the USSR was populated mostly by Ukrainians and Belorussians. Poland's real disaster was the loss of independence and imposing of the communist system on the country for the next 45 years. Poland, now totally dependent on Moscow, stayed economically backward even as compared with such countries as Spain, Greece and Portugal, much poorer than it in the period between the world wars.

Ghetto in 1943 and the Warsaw Uprising in 1944. Both were put down by the Germans. The Soviet army, watching the blood bath in 1944 from the other bank of the Vistula, did not come forward with help. It was Stalin's plan to let the Poles bleed to death in their unequal struggle with the Germans. Only the Western Allies tried to airdrop some weapons and ammunition to the Warsaw insurgents.

The uprising ended in the slaughter of a few hundred thousand inhabitants of Warsaw and the city's total destruction. Altogether, the Second World War claimed about six million casualties in Poland, half of them people of Jewish origin murdered by the Nazis in the ghettos and above all in the concentration camps. Of these camps, Auschwitz will forever remain the symbol of the Holocaust.

Although a member of the victorious coalition, Poland turned out to be one of its most tragic victims. The country's fate was

Unlike in other countries of the socialist bloc, the Soviet Union never managed to bring the communist system in Poland close to any perfection, facing strong resistance of the Polish society. In spite of repression, the

Catholic church survived and even got stronger, becoming a spiritual bastion of the persecuted nation. Also individual farming was saved. Polish culture has been enriched by many excellent artists and authors. The communists were never really able to cut off Polish contacts with the West. Among other reasons, millions of Polish immigrants living in those countries would always support the aspirations of their compatriots in Poland.

Just as in the 19th-century partition period, Poles frequently rose up in rebellion, but armed rising was replaced with worker strikes and demonstrations as well as clandestine conspiracy by the intelligentsia. The first wave of protests in 1956 forced the communists to

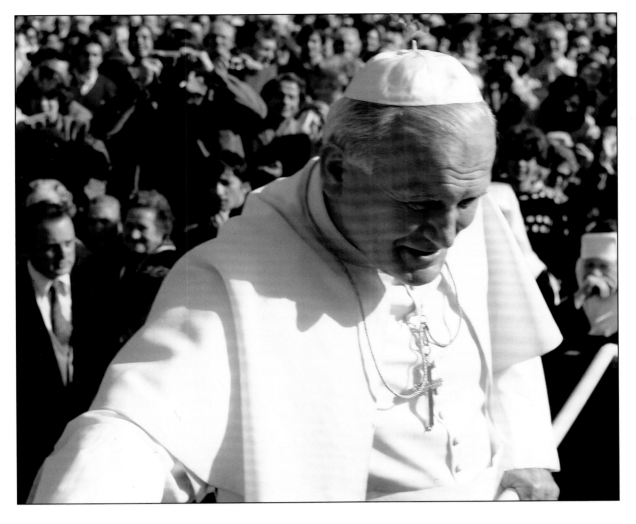

The Polish Pope John Paul II gives spiritual support to the Roman Catholic majority of Polish society

abandon the Stalinist methods of terror. Student riots in 1968 and worker protests in 1970 helped overthrow the autocratic party leader Władysław Gomułka. They also stimulated a superficial opening of the country to Western ways and consumerism by his follower Edward Gierek. After the mass demonstrations of workers in 1976, dissident organizations of the opposition started to act quite openly. More and more underground books and press were published.

Once Again Reborn

It all exploded in August 1980 in the form of the Solidarity movement, started in Gdańsk under the leadership of Lech Wałęsa, which was soon to reach 10 million members. To the amazement and admiration, but also a certain degree of anxiety of the West, Solidarity questioned the whole post-Yalta order with an ever growing courage. This political enthusiasm was closely connected with the election of the Polish Pope, Karol Wojtyła. He visited his homeland as Pope John Paul II a year before the 'Polish August' of 1980 and his visit encouraged the nation. Gathering by the millions at their native Pope's side, Poles could feel their own power.

That was the beginning of the end of communism in Poland. And worldwide, too,

for by a lucky coincidence the new U.S. President Ronald Reagan's personal goal happened to be the dismantling of the Soviet Empire. Though the Soviet system had already disintegrated from within, its fall was accelerated by two events: one, and the most important, was the increase of American armaments, which the USSR could not keep pace with. The other was the birth of the Solidarity union, which provided inspiration for other enslaved countries. Even the introduction of martial law in Poland by General Wojciech Jaruzelski could not stop the clock of history running. Though weakened by countless arrests of its leaders, Solidarity continued to work underground. At that time the underground press became a Polish speciality and the number of book and newspaper titles in illegal, or 'second circulation' amounted to thousands.

In 1989 Poland initiated the new Springtime of Nations in Europe. Pressed by society, the communists agreed to the 'round table' talks with the opposition and to partly free elections. The elections, unprecedented behind the Iron Curtain, ended in the utter failure of the communists. The Polish United Workers' Party, which used to control the government in Poland, was self-dissolved. Still formally a member of the Warsaw Pact, Poland established its first non-communist government headed by Tadeusz Mazowiecki. The government carried out a shock, free-market reform. A year later Lech Wałęsa, an ordinary electrician, was elected president.

Poland was followed by others. The Berlin wall crumbled. The 'peace and socialism bloc' ceased to exist. The USSR collapsed.

Francis Fukuyama announced the end of history. A bit too early, though. The liberal reforms were successful, but they caused a considerable increase in unemployment, unknown to the East-European societies before. Inflation rose and living standards fell for a time. In some countries, including Poland, postcommunists disguised as social democrats or liberals came back to power by means of democratic elections. But this sort of reaction is rather passing and their influence seems to be on the wane. The pendulum of public opinion could be again swinging to the right. The Poles look ahead more trustingly to the future - the Euro-Atlantic future.

Let Some Old Ways Remain

Polish mountains are not as high and majestic as the Alps, but the Tatras, although much lower, match the Alps in the menacing beauty of their rocky crags. The Polish sea is not warm, like the Mediterranean, but its fine beaches are of rare beauty. Siberia has certainly more primeval forests, but the Białowieża Forest (stretching into Belarusan territory) is the grandest of all. Indeed, where else can you meet a huge hairy bison face to face?

Tourists visiting Poland most of all value its naturalness. It is true that two thirds of Poles now live in cities and the country is los-

Corpus Christi procession at Łowicz shows how folk traditions are cherished

ing its fabled idyllic atmosphere, but civilization at its fullest has not yet - fortunately - infected many corners of Poland. To be honest, local inhabitants of such places are less happy about it than visitors from the West.

'Oh, a horse!' my French acquaintance gave a shout of joy every time he saw that animal pulling a plough - a view still quite common in the Polish countryside, though far less common now than a tractor. 'Oh, a hare!' he almost fainted when he saw a grey hare hopping about at leisure next to my country house in the Masurian Lakes. And when he saw a huge plate filled with crayfish freshly pulled out of the River Krutynia, he became nervous, for he calculated that in Paris such a feat would cost him two days' work. And here it was free, fresh from the water.

Hunters - not my favourites - are as excited about coming to Poland as about going on an African safari. Still, they are not bound to see a bear (unless high in the mountains if they are extremely lucky), although many people in the West believe Poland is nothing but snow and bears.

A paradise for ornithologists and bird-watchers it certainly is! Any small village surrounded by marshy meadows can have as many stork nests as the whole of Denmark. They are a distinguishing mark of the Polish countryside. A very rare species of black stork can also be encountered, as well as cormorants, herons and cranes. There are still some wild eagles, though today they are more often seen on the Polish national emblem. The Vistula is an attraction as one of the last unregulated large rivers of Europe. If only its waters were clearer...

Ethnographers and admirers of folklore will find in Poland such rarities as wooden churches and cottages, colourful church festivals and beautiful folk costumes, which have survived only in some regions. It is much worse with folk song tradition, as the young generation now goes in for disco, techno and rock.

One tradition, said to be a national feature of the Poles, is available for every visitor: Polish hospitality. They are particularly

Plaster-of-Paris dwarfs are amassed by the highways leading to the border with Germany

generous in the regions where foreign visitors are not very common, thus being a great attraction for the locals. On the other hand, many border towns in Poland are very hospitable to crowds of visitors from abroad - the Ukraine, Russia, Lithuania, Belarus, the Czech Republic and even Germany - who only come for a day to do their shopping. For them it is cheaper in Poland and everything is in good supply. You can even buy the world's biggest plaster-of-Paris dwarfs - popular garden ornaments in Germany.

Hotels are no longer cheap. Their prices - though not always the services - are now comparable with those in the West. In summer, the most frequented tourist localities offer quite inexpensive rooms and whole houses to let. Bungalows and tents at camping sites or bivouacs are still cheaper. Then let us set out on a journey. For the time being it will be a journey through all the regions of Poland, from the sea to the mountains, shown in the pictures of this book.

19

The Baltic.
The picturesque
seashore at
Dziwnów may
leave the visitor
spellbound

THE GOLDEN
BEACHES COAST

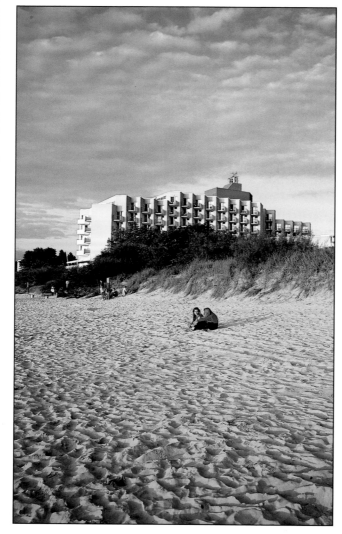

Not many Poles are aware of having their own mini-archipelago: several small islands where the border River Oder flows into the Baltic. They are neither so beautiful nor so extensive as the Canary or Balearic Islands, but the two largest of them - Uznam and Wolin - have some very fashionable beaches at Świnoujście and Międzyzdroje, almost on the border with Germany. A greater part of Uznam belongs to that country, while Poland owns but a tiny eastern area of the island. As long as Poland bordered the German Democratic Republic, the two neighbours kept arguing about a narrow channel in the Baltic leading to Świnoujście port. The argument was accompanied by hostile demonstrations of the 'fraternal' navies. The problem has totally disappeared now that Poland has Federal Germany as its neighbour. Polish relations with the Germans are more friendly than they have ever been since 1000, the year Emperor Otto III paid a visit to Bolesław the Brave at Gniezno. The duke (not yet king) acquired independence from the German church hierarchy and was granted the status of the Emperor's close partner in ruling over the Holy Roman Empire.

The beaches are popular among the Germans and still more among the Swedes, who come here by ferry from Ystad. The south coast

*Międzyzdroje,
a seaside holiday
and health resort*

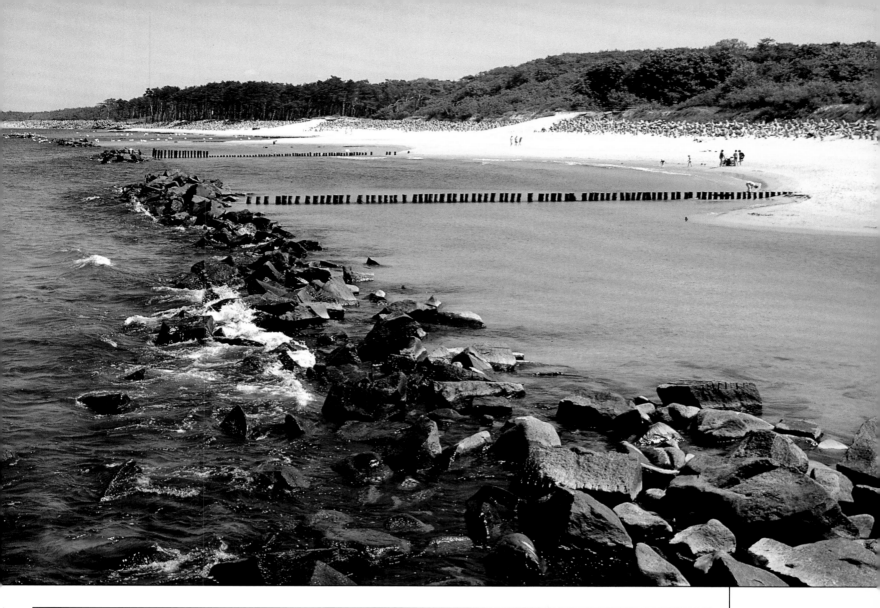

Pobierowo.
Wide, golden
beaches encour-
age one to lie
down

Kamień
Pomorski, an old
port town with an
historic urban
layout. 16th-c.
Town Hall

of the Baltic seems much warmer to the Swedes than to the Poles.

Wolin's attraction is the national park, a habitat of many species of bird, including birds of prey such as the sea eagle. In the 10th century the small fishermen's settlement of Wolin served as an important trading port. According to contemporary chroniclers, it had 12 gates and could allow 300 ships at a time into the harbour. The ships sailed to England, Byzantium and Novgorod. Some Persian coins, Egyptian beads and remains of an old lead glass smelting shop - a great technological achievement for those times - have been excavated in the area by archaeologists. A lighthouse called Vulcan's Pot rose above the port. It lit the way for the Pomeranian tribe of the Wolinianie (Velunzani). After some bitter struggles, they joined the Polish state under the Piasts for a short time. But they mostly formed an alliance with the Slavic federation of the Veleti, spreading westwards nearly as far away as Denmark.

Świnoujście is not only a seaside resort, but primarily it is an outer port of the major city of Szczecin, situated 60 kilometres to the south on the River Oder. Szczecin's connections with Poland were not long-lasting either. The town had its own, pagan dukes. The chronicler Herbord described the local temple of their Three-headed god. When Wolin declined in the 11th century, Szczecin grew into a sizeable and rich port town. It became the seat of the most powerful of all Pomeranian dukedoms. Threatened by German expansionism, this small state maintained friendly relations with Poland. During the period of feudal disintegration it surrendered to the Danes and Brandenburgs . Later it was conquered by the Swedes and Prussians, and even the French during the Napoleonic Wars. And also by the Red Army, which seized Szczecin in the last days of the Second World War to pass it to Poland very reluctantly some time later, plundered and devastated.

Szczecin is distinguished by its urban design modelled in accordance with the solutions of the famous town planner Haussmann during the 19th-century rebuilding of Paris. It is characterized by star-shaped squares with radiating wide avenues lined with trees.

The city, situated on the left bank of the Oder in the north-western distant corner of Poland, is like a gate to the north-European countries. Owing to the rapid development of trade with Germany and the inflow of tourists in recent years, Szczecin has expanded and grown rich. It has become the arena of international life.

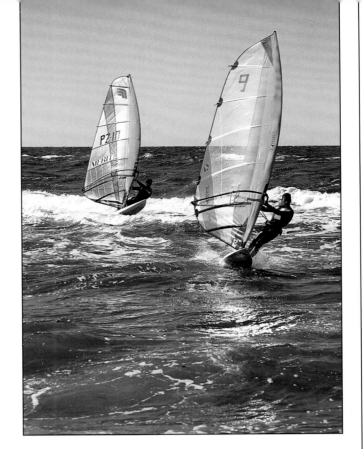

*Trzęsacz.
Ruins of the 15th-c. Gothic church on a high escarpment, washed away by the sea*

*Dziwnówek.
Polish Windsurfing Championships*

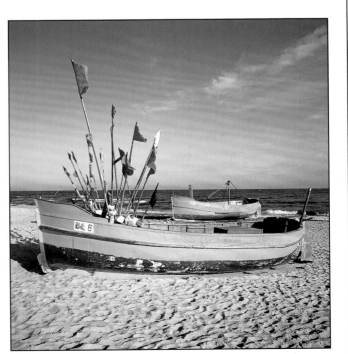

*Mielno,
a holiday resort by the seaside*

*Rewal.
Fishing boats*

*Gryfice.
High Gate,
a fragment of the
medieval de-
fence walls*

*Koszalin,
one of the richest
Pomeranian
towns in the
14th c. Market
square with the
Gothic St. Mary's
Church*

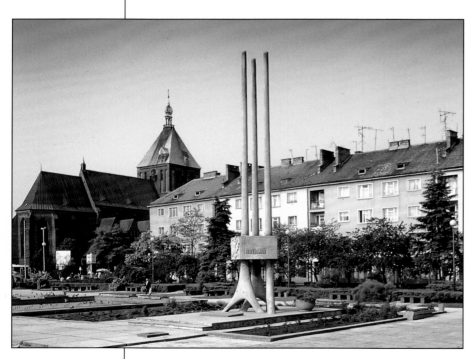

Opposite Wolin Island on the right bank of the River Dziwna, which in fact is a strait, lies the little old town of Kamień Pomorski. In the past it was also the seat of a duke and a bishop. In the Romanesque-Gothic cathedral internationally renowned festivals of organ and chamber music are held. East of Kamień Pomorski, 400 kilometres of wonderful beaches stretch along the seashore. The sea is not azure but usually grey, nevertheless to many artists, especially marine painters, it looks exceptionally beautiful. They prefer the soft palette of sand dunes overgrown with pine trees bent and twisted by the wind to the bright colours of the Riviera or the lifeless symmetry of Levant cypresses. This landscape is more like graphic art than painting. Even the clear sky has less glow than in the Mediterranean and when it becomes cloudy, you can really feel the severity of the northern seas. If you prefer Bruegel to Gaugin, you are bound to fall in love with the Baltic.

A line of fishing villages and tourist resorts string along the never-ending strand of beaches. Each place has its devotees: Dziwnowo, Pobierowo, Rewal, Niechorze, Mrzeżyno and Trzęsacz on a high cliff washed away by sea waves, so that the old Gothic church once a mile away from the sea, now has almost completely collapsed into the Baltic. The nearby town of Kołobrzeg is a popular health resort, frequented by Swedish tourists. The town, dating from the 8th century, was the seat of one of the first Polish bishoprics from 1000. During the Second World War, after fierce fighting, Kołobrzeg was captured by the troops of the 1st Polish Army coming together with the Red

*Darłowo.
Market square
with the Baroque
Town Hall and the
Gothic church*

*Białogard,
an old Slavic
settlement.
A burgher's
house in the
market square*

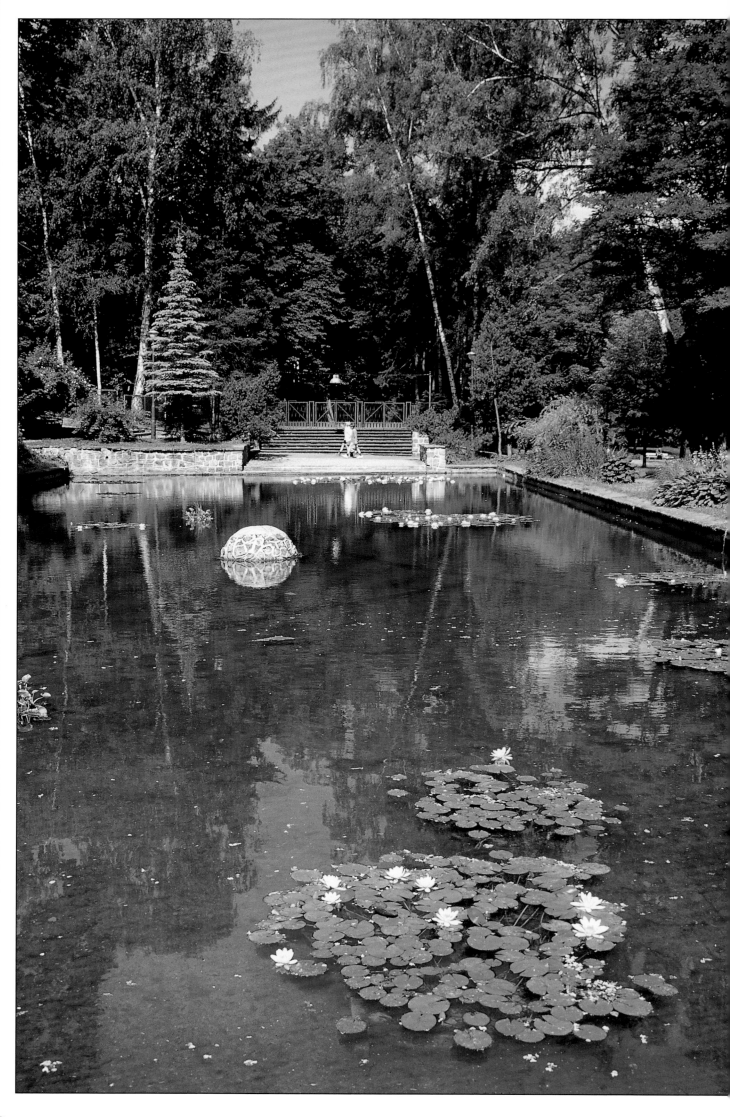

Połczyn Zdrój, a holiday and health resort with a fine spa park

Świdwin.
The Gothic Castle
built on the site
of a former Slavic
settlement

Army. The town was nearly totally destroyed. Fortunately, after the war it was reconstructed and made a real town of gardens by its young and enthusiastic architects.

More summer resorts are found further to the east: Ustronie Morskie, Sarbinowo and Mielno, Unieście on the sandbar between the sea and Lake Jamno, the fishing port of Darłowo, Jarosławiec, and the most favoured: Ustka and Łeba. The two towns are engaged in a seething dispute about which of them deserves the title of the summer capital of Poland. As a matter of fact, both do.

The Słowiński National Park begins on the outskirts of Łeba. The main attraction in the park are mobile high dunes, the highest of which, at Czołpin, rises up to 56 metres. They form a true desert in miniature. The sand travels with the wind, fighting a victorious battle against the plant life. Wide expanses of forest have already fallen victim to it. The nearby large Lake Łebsko with its shores dense with vegetation and famous for its multitude of water birds, is excellent for sailing. Some more coastal lakes, divided from the sea by narrow strips of land, lie in the neighbourhood. The village of Kluki, formerly owned by one large family, the Kluks, has a *skansen* museum of the Slovincian people, a small Pomeranian tribe which managed to resist Germanization and keep its own language till the early 20th century. Some fisherman families claim to have Slovincian ancestry even though they cannot speak their language any more, although they have learnt to speak Polish.

A line of smaller and bigger coastal towns has developed from medieval settlements built at a safe distance from the sea. The very sea shore, plundered by the Scandinavian pirates called Vikings, was too dangerous to settle. The history of such towns as Gryfice, Białogard, Koszalin, Sławno and Lębork dates back to the Middle Ages. Fragments of sacral buildings and

Szczecinek, a centre of water tourism between lakes Wielimie and Trzesiecko. Fragment of the town architecture

Lake Trzesiecko near Szczecinek. Yacht harbour

fortifications from that time have been preserved. Słupsk, apart from its historic monuments, has also made a name for its excellent 'Słupsk inns', in which the tradition of Slovincian and Kashubian cuisine is carried on. Similar inns with fine stylized interiors have been opened in other Polish towns and some of their ornamental elements are even sold abroad.

The region to the south, called the Pomeranian Lake District - unlike the Masurian Lake District - has not yet been discovered by tourists. It was not until a few years ago that large areas of this region, including forests, lakes and towns, became accessible to Poles. Some old towns were not even shown on any map. These were the territories of Soviet troops stationing in Poland - their bases and military train-

Złocieniec, a town amid the forests and small lakes. One side of the market square

Drawsko Pomorskie. Bestiaries baked in brick in the side portal of the 14th-c. church

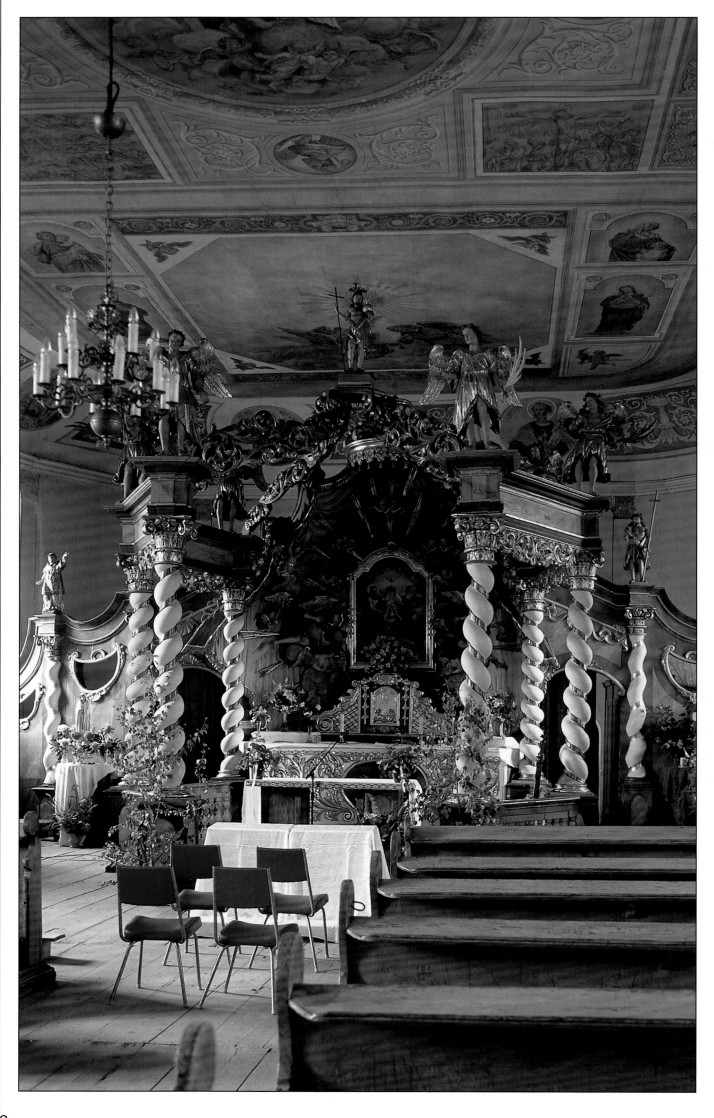

Czaplinek, the centre of the Drawsko Lake District. 18th-c. canopy altar in the Gothic church

ing grounds. When the Warsaw Pact was dissolved and the Soviet Army left for Russia in 1992, the Poles were astonished to learn that they had a new town: Borne-Sulinowo. Until then a secret locality, it was left deserted. A lot of people, especially the young and homeless, came to settle here, but in order to live they also needed jobs. Year by year, the Polish Far West has slowly been adapting to a normal life. Country houses and camping sites have appeared on newly acquired lakes; you can pick blackberries in former 'no access' forests. You must be very cautious, though, not to step on a land mine or a grenade.

The Drawsko Lake District is unusually picturesque. Its beautifully situated health resort, Połczyn Zdrój is known for its mild climate and curative mineral water. The Bytów Lake District is almost equally charming. The largest lake of the region is Miedwie near Szczecin. Its bottom is as deep as 28 metres below sea level.

Lake Drawsko, the second deepest in Poland, has picturesque bays and forms part of the Drawsko Landscape Park

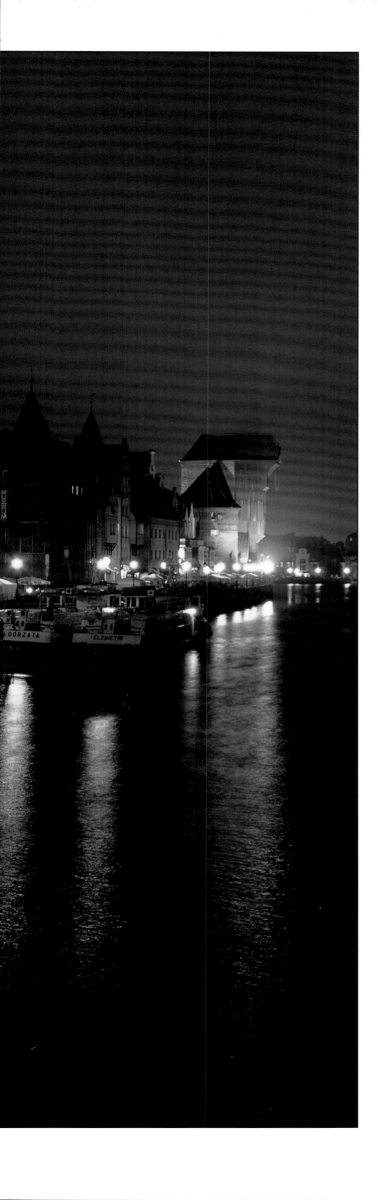

THE LAND OF
AMBER AND
COPERNICUS

Ciechocinek, a famous spa since the 19th c. Wooden graduation tower and a flower clock in the Spa Park

The Vistula widens into the Włocławek Reservoir in front of a great dam, which was meant to start the 'cascadization' of the river. Several other dams with sluice-gates and water turbines were planned. From lack of funds, the first dam was the only one constructed. Some claim it is just good for the Vistula, which has remained the wildest river in Europe, to the advantage of tourists, anglers and ornithologists, as well as all aesthetes and traditionalists.

In no circumstances should you miss Ciechocinek, the most famous saline spa in Poland. In the early 19th century three graduation towers for brine were constructed here: huge wooden frames packed with branches. Brine flows down the branches and salt is deposited. The area around, saturated with salt and iodine molecules and when it is sunny also healthy ozone, forms a kind of gigantic inhalation site. Apart from their medicinal properties, the towers are a unique example of such construction in the world.

Going down the Vistula we arrive in Toruń, a town closely associated with Nicolaus Copernicus. Suddenly we are in the Middle Ages. The entire old centre of Toruń is a historic monument of international rank and there is no other Gothic town like this in Poland.

The well-preserved town hall was built in the 13th/14th centuries and slightly rebuilt at the beginning of the 17th century in the Mannerist style by the famous Dutch architect A. van Obbergen. Close by at 17 Kopernika (Copernicus) Street the greatest astronomer of all times was born in 1473. Although he wrote in German or Latin, he always considered himself a Pole. He was also a physician, administrator, mathematician, economist and canon. The Church, however, strongly objected to his heliocentric concept of the universe and pronounced it to be dangerous for the religious outlook, although it was accepted by such scholars as Giordano Bruno, Galileo and Kepler. His work *De revolutionibus...* was not removed from the index of forbidden books until 1757. From that year on the Earth could continue going round the Sun without committing a sin.

Other treasures of Gothic architecture include the 13th-century St. John's Church with its beautiful authentic wall paintings, the early-14th-century monumental Basilica of St. James, and the oldest of them - the Church of the Virgin Mary. Fragments of defence walls as well as numerous gates, bastions and towers have been preserved in Toruń.

Only 50 kilometres away from Toruń lies the rival town of Bydgoszcz, the biggest river port in Poland. Here, via a canal, the Vistula system is connected with the inland water routes of Western Europe. In the Polish transport system, river navigation plays a marginal role, though. Bydgoszcz is larger than Toruń and its beginning dates back to the 13th cen-

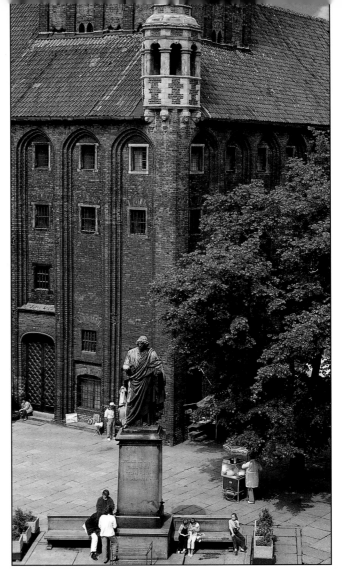

Toruń, an old Hanseatic town with many historic relics. Nicolaus Copernicus Monument with the Gothic Town Hall in the background and Szeroka Street in the Old Town with a view of the 18th-c. Church of the Holy Spirit

Bydgoszcz on the Brda, a 15th and 16th-c. centre of grain and salt trade. Urban architecture on the river bank

tury. The town's historic places include the late-Renaissance Church of the Poor Clares and a complex of 18th-century granaries.

On the Nogat, a branch of the Vistula, towers the huge castle-monastery of Malbork, the main stronghold and capital of the Teutonic state. A great attraction for tourists, it was about the greatest fortress built in medieval Europe.

The Żuławy region in the delta of the Vistula between the river branches has the best alluvial soil in Poland, deposited by the Vistula. The region, lying below sea level, was

Malbork. Castle courtyard cloister

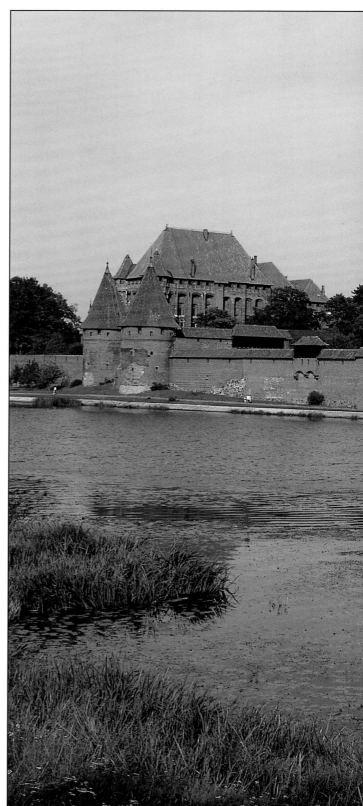

often flooded in the past, when people did not know how to build strong embankments. Elbląg, a town at the east edge of the Żuławy, had unsuccessfully competed with Gdańsk in the Baltic trade before it lost its importance as a port.

Gdańsk is one of three cities in Poland, next to Warsaw and Cracow, which have a worldwide reputation. There are two reasons for that. The first reason is that here in Gdańsk the first shots in the Second World War were fired by the German training battleship *Schleswig-Holstein* at 4.45 am on 1st September 1939. The shots were directed at the Polish military post and depot on the Westerplatte Peninsula - a Polish enclave within the territory of the Free City of Danzig under the pro-visions of the Treaty of Versailles. The city was officially supervised by the League of Nations, but in fact it had come under the control of the Nazis. The Polish outpost, manned by 182 soldiers, resisted the attacks from land, sea and air by twenty times stronger German forces for a whole week. The Battle of Westerplatte is now given in history textbooks as an example of Polish soldiers' greatest deeds.

Another reason for Gdańsk's popular-ity was the far-famed strike in the Gdańsk Shipyard led by Lech Wałęsa. It started on 14 August 1980 and resulted in the first ever agreement made between the government and the protesting workers in the history of communist countries, as well as the forma-

Malbork, a town set up by the Teutonic Knights on the Nogat. The castle built in the 13th-15th c., one of the most outstanding examples of medieval fortification architecture

Gdańsk, a historic port with magnificent old architecture. Długi Targ Street, teeming with life despite the late hour

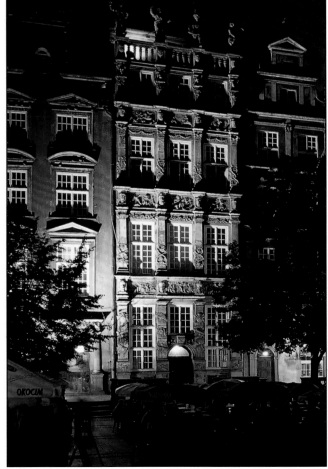

Gdańsk. House façades on Długi Targ floodlit in the evening

tion of the Solidarity union. More strikes in 1988 effected in the 'round table' talks of the communists with their political adversaries. The talks enhanced the triumph of democracy in Poland and other countries of Eastern Europe. In those years Gdańsk was the main bastion of Polish opposition and it is still the headquarters of the Independent, Self-administered Trade Union Solidarity.

Naturally, the history of Gdańsk and its region began much earlier - two thousand years ago. The Polish nation did not yet exist. The land, populated by numerous proto-Slavic and Baltic tribes, was visited by caravans of merchants from as far away as ancient Rome. According to Pliny, the first of them was sent by the cruel emperor Nero himself, who got so enchanted by a light yellowish stone he saw on a slave woman's alluring bosom, that he arranged a great expedition to the 'northern barbarians'. Bold merchants crossed the Alps, then the Danube at Vindobona (today Vienna), and arrived at the settlement of Calisia (today the town of Kalisz), where they bought some amber. As it was too little for the emperor's court's needs, they proceeded further, crossed the Vistula (which in English has retained the Latin name) and reached the present Gdańsk area, or maybe as far as the Sambia Peninsula, which isn't in Poland.

A small village could have existed at the present site of Gdańsk as early as the 9th or even 8th century. However, at that time a mysterious port of Truso, described by traveller Wulfstan, dominated in the region and grew into a mighty settlement in the 10th century, only to disappear without trace. It might have lain somewhere on a deep gulf which later formed Lake Drużno, reportedly the richest in birds of all lakes in Europe.

At about that time, in *The Life of St. Adalbert*, dated 997, a name of unknown origin and difficult to pronounce appeared: Gyddanyzc. Modified into Kdanzc and then Gdantz, it finally became Danzig in German and Gdańsk in Polish.

It was already a big and cosmopolitan city, inhabited by Pomeranians and Poles, then also by some Germans and numerous Flemish, Scottish and other settlers from the West. Gdańsk was a member of the Hanseatic League, which exercised a great commercial and military power over the North Sea and the Baltic. During the Polish-Teutonic wars the dwellers of Gdańsk, though to a great degree Germanized, were on the side of Poland and drove the Teutonic Knights away. It turned to be a profitable move, for Poland was becoming a leading exporter of farm produce and forest crops in Europe. Goods were floated along the Vistula to Gdańsk. The town grew rich and expanded in the fine Flemish style. It became a major centre of culture, science and printing. Gdańsk astronomer Johan Hevelius, honoured with awards by Louis XIV of France, Charles II of England and the Pope, was famed all over Europe. Gabriel Fahrenheit, the inventor of a thermometer, also started his career in Gdańsk. After the first partition of Poland in 1772, Gdańsk remained part of Poland - an enclave separated from it by the Prussian partition zone (almost like a free city).

Gdańsk. Panorama of the historic Main Town with the largest Polish hall church, the 14th/15th-c. St. Mary's, towering above the merchant and burghers' houses; the Neptune Fountain and the Gothic Main Town Hall closing the perspective of Długa Street

Most of Gdańsk's inhabitants were Protestants and spoke German, but they felt offended if someone called them Prussians. They regarded themselves simply as Gdańsk people - the city was their homeland.

For the first time Gdańsk was given the status of a free city under Napoleon Bonaparte, who visited it in 1807 after the seizure of the town from Prussian hands and was enthusiastically greeted. A similar status, though not granted officially, had been enjoyed by Gdańsk under Polish kings. After the fall of Napoleon Gdańsk went back to Prussia and became an ordinary, provincial town. It became a free city again between the First and the Second World Wars. Regained by Poland in 1945, it was all in ruins. In a few years it was rebuilt with great care and attention to its historic architecture, mostly Gothic and the Flemish Mannerism. The Gdańsk Old

Gdynia, together with Gdańsk and Sopot constitutes the Tri-city, a major port and centre of maritime economy. Monument to Joseph Conrad (J. K. Korzeniowski) at the end of the South Pier

Town is a beautiful place for sightseeing, especially the Long Market route from the Golden Gate to the Green Gate (a remainder of the defence walls standing in the old port on the Motława), with unique restored medieval granaries. The main sacred building is the monumental Gothic Church of the Holy Virgin Mary.

The former health resort of Sopot, with a casino almost as famous as that in Monte Carlo, today serves as a summer mecca for all Poles, especially during the International Song Festival held every summer at the Forest Opera.

The third city, Gdynia, is completely different. It was built in the early 1920s along with the port, which at the end of the following decade was already the busiest harbour in the Baltic Sea.

When the weather is fine, the view from the hills around the Tri-city extends as far as the Hel Peninsula, a 30-kilometre-long narrow stretch of land resembling a scythe, which, like many villages south of the Tri-city, is inhabited by the Kashubians, the remainder of the old Pomeranian tribe, who resisted a thousand years of Germanization and Polonization to preserve their own dialect, hardly understandable to Poles.

Another narrow sandbar with many bathing beaches in the vicinity of Gdańsk lies at the Vistula mouth, separating the Baltic Sea from the Vistula Lagoon.

*Mikołajki
on Lake
Mikołajskie
in the Masurian
Lake District,
a water sport and
holiday centre*

FINLAND IN MINIATURE

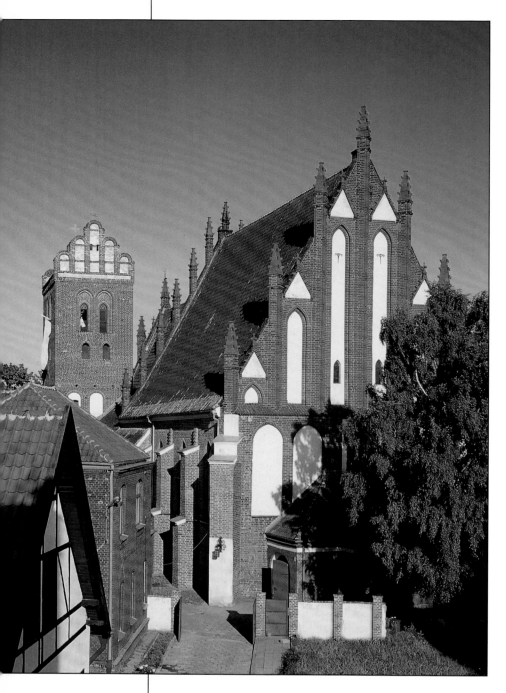

Other countries have higher mountains, warmer seas and more ancient historic relics than Poland. But such an amassment of lakes as in the Masuria (Mazury) is hardly met in any other country in Europe west of Russia and south of Finland.

The lakes are of various types. The largest, Lake Śniardwy (109 km^2) looks like a little sea with dangerous crested waves. There are a lot of smaller lakes of the same type, with countless bays, promontories and islets. There are still more long and narrow ribbon lakes and innumerous tiny pools entirely hidden in woods, dense shrubs or reeds.

Connected by small rivers and canals, they form a vast system of lakes, which can be sailed along for weeks on end without returning once to the same place. Altogether, the Masurian Lake District consists of 1370 lakes of more than one hectare in area.

Masuria is the greatest tourist attraction in Poland. The lakes are surrounded by a hilly post-glacial landscape formed by moraines, with vast meadows bathed in flowers. The local forests abound in wildlife (boar, elk, red deer and roe-deer, not to mention all kinds of small game). You will find old castles, isolated villages in the middle of the forest and other remote and mysterious places 'where God lost his shoes'.

Olsztyn is the main city of the Masurian Lake District. It is the capital of Warmia, a historic region inseparably tied with Masuria.

*Iława
on Lake Jeziorak.
Gothic Church of
the Transfigura-
tion*

*Lake Jeziorak.
Yacht harbour
at Iława*

*Ostróda
on Lake
Drwęckie,
a centre of water
tourism. Frag-
ment of the town
with the Gothic
church*

*Miłomłyn
near Ostróda.
Ostróda-Elbląg
Canal*

Grunwald, the battlefield where the Teutonic Knights were defeated in 1410, with Grunwald Monument

Barczewo. Gothic Town Hall, remodelled in the 19th c.

*Olsztyn
on the Łyna in the
Olsztyn Lake
District, the main
city of the Warmia
and Masuria
regions. 17th-c.
Town Hall and
Staromiejska
Street*

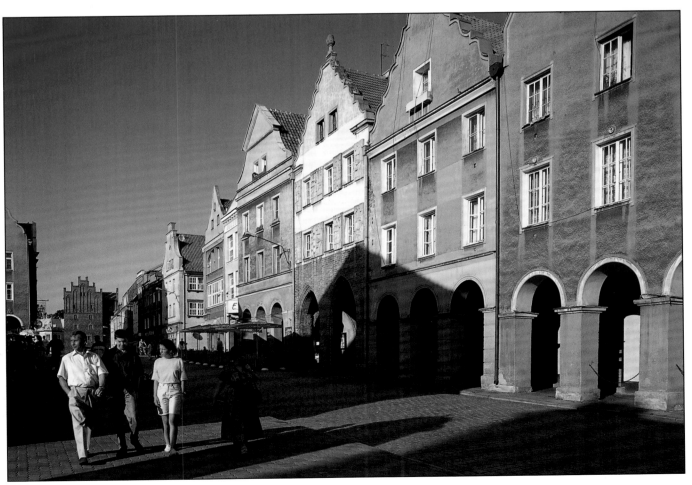

Warmia belonged to Poland for several centuries and remained Roman Catholic. Masuria was not an integral part of Poland, only a vassal province. Quite paradoxically the Masurian people, the majority of whom were members of Evangelical Church, stuck obsessively to the Polish speech. Maybe it was because they descended from some Mazovian settlers. Until recently, a few village communities of Mormones lived in Masuria.

Back in the past, at the beginning of the second millennium, Warmia and Masuria were inhabited not by Slavs, but by the Baltic tribes of Pruthenians and Sudovians, related to today's Lithuanians and Latvians. The Sudovians, a militant people constantly both-

ering its neighbours, were defeated and almost completely assimilated or killed off by the combined forces of the Teutonic Knights, Poles, Lithuanians and Ruthenians at the end of the 13th century. The remainder were deported to distant lands, for instance to Mazovia. A few place names and surnames are now their only reminder. The Pruthenians, or Prussians, were Germanized. In exchange for that, their conquerors in knightly robes ornamented with a black cross had their state named Prussia. It developed into one of the strongest and most aggressive of all German states.

The medieval castle in Olsztyn is beautifully situated on the bank of the Łyna, near

*Biskupiec
in the Mrągowo
Lake District.
19th-c. houses in
the market
square*

Lidzbark Warmiński. Inside the Castle of the Bishops of Warmia, now the Warmia Museum, and the Gothic altar in the Parish Church

St. James's Cathedral and some fragments of the defence walls. The castle once belonged to the chapter of the Teutonic Knights at Frombork. Olsztyn Castle was administered by Nicolaus Copernicus in the years 1515-21. As a true Renaissance man, he did not restrict his sphere of interest to astronomy. Among his many skills, including writing poetry, he was an efficient administrator and good economist. He formulated the law that 'bad money drives out good' earlier than Gresham.

He also proved to be a brilliant strategist, successfully defending the castle from the Teutonic Knights.

Today Olsztyn is far from being only a tourist attraction. It has a big tyre factory and the three adjacent lakes are not fit for bathing. But only several kilometres away the lakes are suitable not only for people but also for crayfish, creatures very sensitive to water pollution.

Lidzbark Warmiński, a seat of the Warmia Bishops from the mid-14th c. Gothic castle on a square plan with a courtyard and four corner towers

The region west of Olsztyn, known as the Iława-Ostróda Lake District, has the large and twisted Lake Jeziorak as well as the interesting Elbląg Canal with its famous locks, where boats must be raised or lowered from one water level to the other. In the south of this region lies the village of Grunwald, where the most widely acclaimed battle with the Teutonic Knights took place in 1410. King Władysław Jagiełło and his cousin, Duke Witold of Lithuania, crushed the army of the Grand Master Ulrich von Jungingen. Military historians have conducted thorough studies of this battle. Many strategic tricks used by King Władysław have been described, such as pretended escaping, flanking manoeuvres or using cavalry in the decisive phase of the battle - all of them picked up by the king from the Tartars.

In the east the Masurian Lake District neighbours on another lake district in the Suwałki region, in the distant past inhabited by the above mentioned Sudovians. According to many connoisseurs, this area of hilly

Święta Lipka, the Baroque Jesuit monastic complex. The Church of the Visitation of the Holy Virgin Mary; inside – a Baroque organ with movable parts

The most beautiful region, 100 kilometres east of Olsztyn, is called the 'Land of Great Lakes'. Śniardwy, Mamry, Bełdan, Niegocin, Roś and some smaller lakes together amount to 350 square kilometres of water surface. The main, well-equipped holiday centres are Mikołajki, Giżycko, Węgorzewo and Ruciane. Pleasure boats run from one lake port to another for those who prefer comfort rather than struggling with stays. Canoeing is most attractive on the enchanting meanders of the crystal clear River Krutynia.

What about some skiing? Snow stays quite long over the Masurian land and its diversified topography provides ideal conditions for cross-country skiing. The Szeskie and Dylewskie Hills, more than 300 metres in height, offer good slopes for Alpine skiing, though perhaps not for ambitious skiers, while for iceboaters Masuria is a paradise.

A zoological curiosity, wild small forest horses are bred at Popielno on Lake Śniardwy in order to reproduce the species of tarpan, extinct since the 19th century.

Beavers, once close to extinction, now proliferate, driving the local farmers to despair, for the beavers' dams cause the flooding of their fields. Some muddy lakes provide habitat for a rare species of swamp turtle.

54

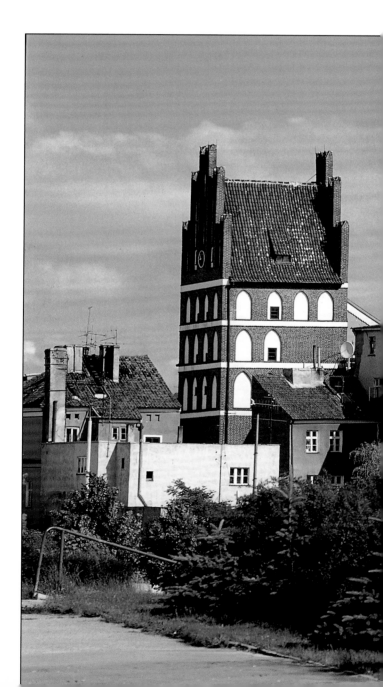

land dotted with lakes on various heights, especially near Smolniki, is the most beautiful part of Poland. Perhaps they are right. Wigry being the most popular of the district's lakes, Hańcza is a natural wonder: the deepest lake in Poland (109 m) with elevated shores overgrown with forest. Through this lake flows the small river Czarna Hańcza, in its beauty surpassing even the famous Krutynia.

A local curiosity is the Orthodox Church community, who have been living in several local villages for three centuries. They continue to speak Russian and observe the strict principles of their faith. They marry within the community, though the young generation are now starting to break away. They never shave and they baptize their children by immersing them three times, head included, in cold water straight from a well.

A few thousand Lithuanians live near the town of Sejny and the village of Puńsk close to the Lithuanian border. They have their own schools and folk bands, and enjoy all the rights that ethnic minorities are entitled to.

Stoczek Klasztorny, the Marist Monastery. Interior of the Church of Our Lady of Peace

Bartoszyce. View of the town with the Gothic Lidzbark Gate and St. Nicholas' Church

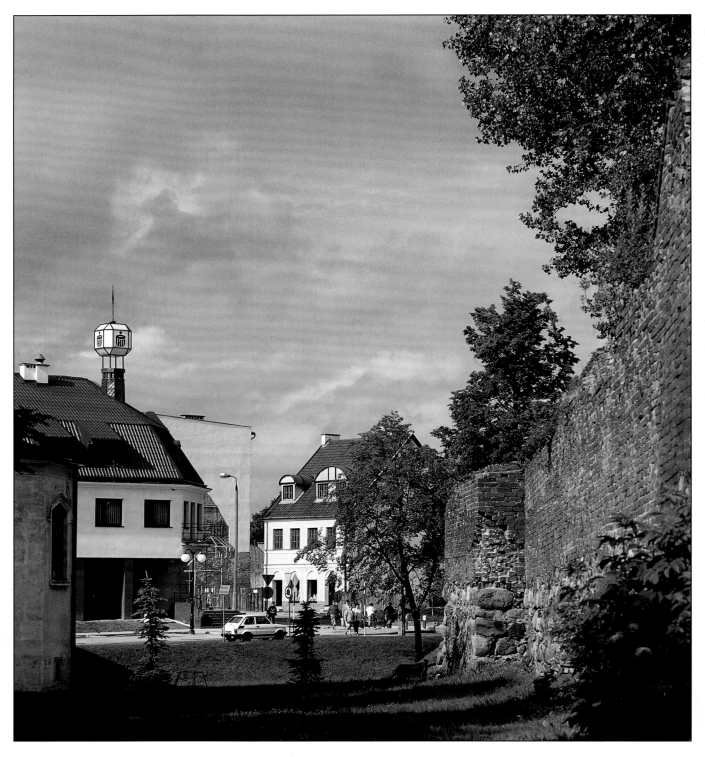

Kętrzyn,
an old Prussian
settlement and
later the Teu-
tonic Knights'
town, situated
near the former
headquarters of
Hitler in the
bunkers at
Gierłoża. Partial
view of the town

The nearby vast Augustów Forest is also embellished with a series of beautiful lakes: Niecko, Białe, Studzieniczne, Sajno and the more distant Serwy. They are connected by natural passages and a canal with 18 sluices, built between 1825 and 1834. It was meant to form part of the route for exporting Polish goods to Windau (now Ventspils in Latvia) after the traditional route along the Vistula to Gdańsk had been cut off by the Prussian customs border. Later, when railways were introduced, water routes lost their importance. The canal was designed and its construction was supervised by General Ignacy Prądzyński, a great strategist who made a name for himself during the November Insurrection in

Mrągowo,
a holiday resort
famous for the
'Picnic Country'
Festivals.
A backwater of
the town

1830. Today the canal, no longer used for commercial purposes, is a precious historic monument of Polish engineering and also a wonderful route for water tourism.

Szczytno.
The castle built on the foundations of its Gothic destroyed predecessor, now housing the Museum of Masuria

Białowieża Forest, part of the Białowieża National Park considered by UNESCO as a biosphere reserve. Spring anemones in the forest

PODLASIE, THE BACKWOODS OF POLAND

*Białowieża,
a village
in the Białowieża
Forest. Orthodox
church; preparing wood for fuel*

The first impression is 'dark and wet', like in a primeval forest. And such a forest it is. The Białowieża Forest, the last great natural forest complex in Europe (outside Russia), has still some areas of virgin forest untouched by man. In the strict-reserve territory of the Białowieża National Park the lynx, wild boar, red deer and elk play host to visitors. The fauna sometimes includes a wolf or brown bear - illegally slipping across the 'green border' with Belarus.

But the lord of the forest is the bearded and horned, mighty European bison.

An average male of this splendid animal, weighing about a thousand kilograms, would make the American bison look like some weakling. The species became extinct after the First World War, having been killed for food. Not a single specimen was left in the Białowieża Forest, once its largest habitat. Fortunately for the bison, an international commission for its protection was set up with the active participation of Poland. Individual animals were purchased from various zoos - some of them were mixed with the Caucasian bison - and the researchers at Białowieża began to work on the restitution of the spe-

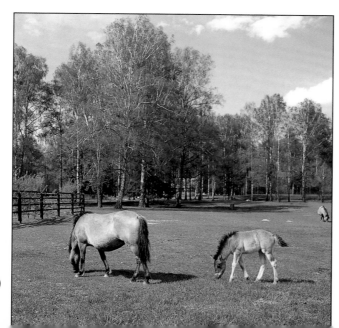

*Białowieża.
Tarpans in the
reserve*

*Białowieża.
19th-c. romantic
park around the
palace*

*Hajnówka,
a village at the
outskirts of
Białowieża Forest.
Modern Orthodox
Church of the
Holy Trinity*

Bielsk Podlaski, former Russian castle town destroyed by the Tartars. Town Hall with a Baroque tower

Siemianówka Reservoir, an artificial lake on the Narew

cies. Today the number of bison in the Białowieża Forest amounts to 300, most of them living at liberty. As they were becoming short of space in the Białowieża Forest, some bison were transferred to other forests. The species has been saved and now the weaker specimens may even be hunted for - under the strict control of researchers and foresters and for a fat fee of tens of thousands dollars.

The whole Białowieża Forest has an area of 1250 square kilometres, of which nearly 600 belong to Poland. The forest provides a natural research laboratory for all kinds of naturalists. It abounds in many species of ancient trees several centuries in age. Almost all types of forest once overgrowing the North European Plain have been preserved here.

Roaming the backwoods of Białowieża is by no means a safe and simple walk. It is quite an adventure, and a risky one unless you are an experienced hiker. Good orientation is needed not to get lost in the tangle of growing and fallen trees or get stuck in some boggy hollow. It may happen that an old rot-

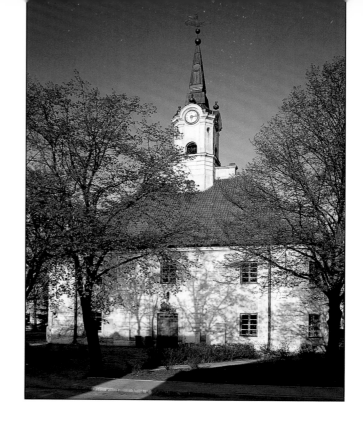

ten tree falls down all of a sudden with a bang. Wild, untamed nature! But if you meet a bison - do not panic. Even if it steps on the road to have a look at cars and people, it will soon with great dignity withdraw to the wood.

990 species of plants have been registered in the Białowieża, not counting microflora. As much as 200 of them are lichens. Animal species amount to 11 000, three quarters of which are insects. 228 species of birds include the eagle, falcon, capercaillie and black grouse.

Another intact natural habitat, less known even to Poles, extends over the lowlands on the winding River Biebrza. The vast marshland, a true nature paradise, is now quite unique in Western Europe. Even elks roam this wet terrain, and beavers seem to like it. Before and after the Second World War the Biebrza Marshes were in danger of being drained by land reclamation engineers, bent on making every wet place dry. The Biebrza valley was lucky: the protracted argument between engineers and ecologists was won by the latter and the Biebrza National Park was established. Its unique character is marked by complete inaccessibility of the marshes and peatbogs in the autumn and spring. They can be entered neither on foot nor by boat. Countless pools, little canals and old river beds swarm with fish, but in order to go angling there it would be necessary to pass through treacherous swamps.

Białystok on the Biała. 15th-c. historic city centre with a Baroque house and neo-Gothic church; in the chapel of the Branicki Palace, one of the finest palace-cum-garden complexes in Poland

Czarna Białostocka surrounded by Knyszyn Forest. Orthodox church in the Buksztel district

The whole Podlasie region is called 'Poland B', which means inferior to the central and western parts of the country. It has poor, sandy soils, almost no industry and high unemployment. Not only its geographical situation, but also the local lifestyles and living standards place Podlasie closer to Belarus than to Central Europe.

And a lot of Belorussians, mostly Orthodox, live in the vicinity of the Białowieża Forest. They have their own holy hill, Grabarka, to which they make annual summer pilgrimages. They come from all directions carrying crosses - slightly different from the Roman Catholic ones - and chanting beautifully to

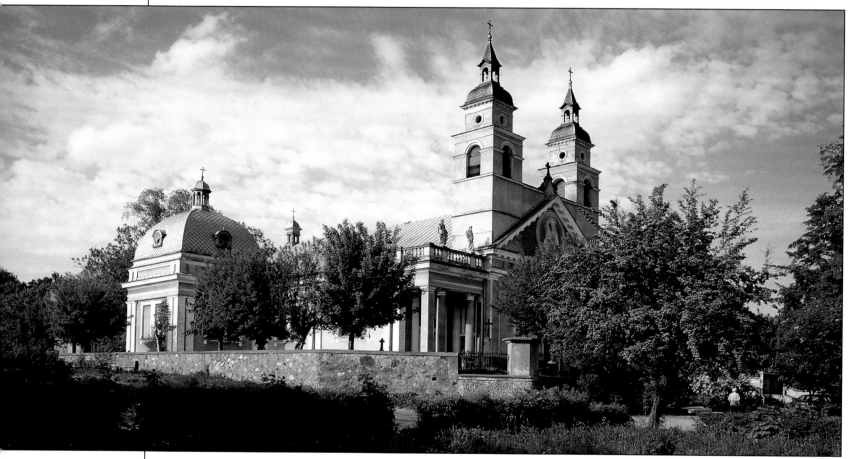

Sokółka, once a forest settlement of the Lithuanian dukes. Neoclassical Parish Church

Tykocin. Baroque synagogue, now a museum

God. It is one of the most mystic and exotic religious ceremonies performed in Poland.

With a bit of luck you may also hear a muezzin singing in this country. In the villages Bohoniki and Kruszyniany some descendants of King John III Sobieski's Tartar soldiers still bow down before Allah in their two historic mosques, reciting the verses of the Koran in the Arabic language they can no longer understand. Much more Tartars used to live in Poland before the Second World War. They even formed a Tartar cavalry squadron in the Polish army.

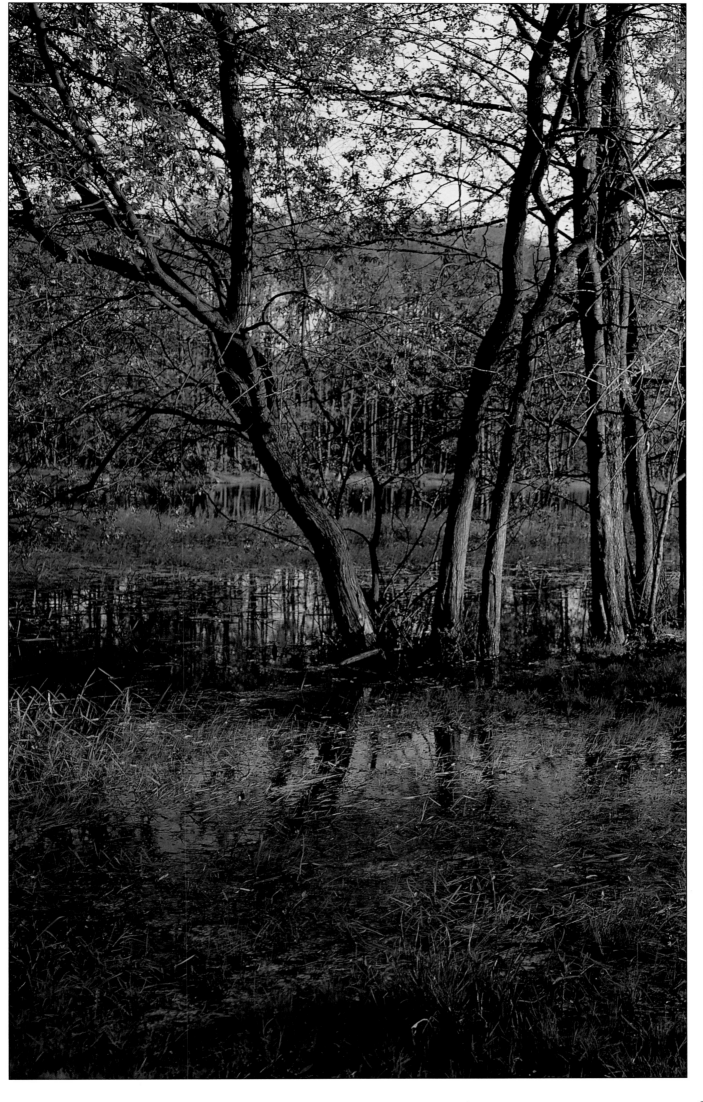

The Narew.
Flood waters of
the unregulated
river

Natural forests in the Biebrza Valley, part of the Biebrza National Park

*Rajgród,
medieval town of
the Sudovians.
Interior of the
neo-Gothic Parish
Church*

Ethnographers will perhaps take some
interest in the so called 'villages of the nobles'
in the Podlasie region, inhabited by descendants of the small landed gentry, equivalent to
British yeomen. Although their life and
wealth (or rather lack of it) at present is no
different from that of their peasant neighbours, they are still proud of their noble origin, names and traditions. They boast their
family coats of arms and swagger into the
church on Sunday feeling better than the rest

*Grajewo –
19th-c. church
and belfry*

Drozdowo near Łomża. Natural History Museum

*Łomża
on the high
Narew escarp-
ment, a town from
the 14th c.
The market square*

of the villagers. About sixty years or so ago it could still happen that a Podlasie nobleman ploughed his field carrying his curved sword strapped to his waist. In more recent times, his daughters had to wear gloves when pulling up weeds in the flowerbeds or milking cows. Maybe they still do?

Where there is nobility, there are horses. The stud-farm at Janowiec Podlaski has been keeping thoroughbred Arab horses for nearly two hundred years. Millionaires from all over the world attend its horse auctions every year.

The rural character of the Podlasie region is a tourist attraction in itself, for such pristine landscapes are hardly seen any more in modern and rich areas. Białystok, the main city of the region, has expanded in the last decades. This otherwise commonplace city has one gem: the Branicki Palace designed by Tylman van Gameren in the 17th century. One of the most beautiful Baroque palaces in Poland, it is locally called 'the Podlasie Versailles'. Not without reason: among the guests of the Branicki Palace were some members of the royal Bourbon family who managed to escape the Jacobinic guillotine. Today the palace houses the Medical Academy.

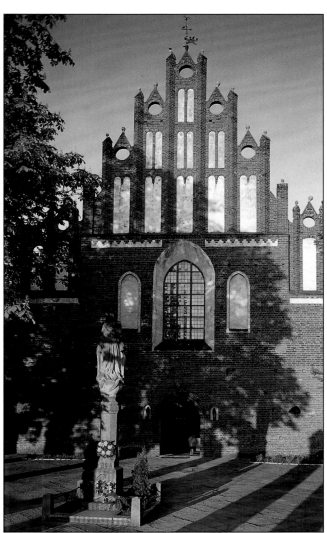

*Wizna,
a village at the
confluence of the
Biebrza and the
Narew. Late-
Gothic Parish
Church*

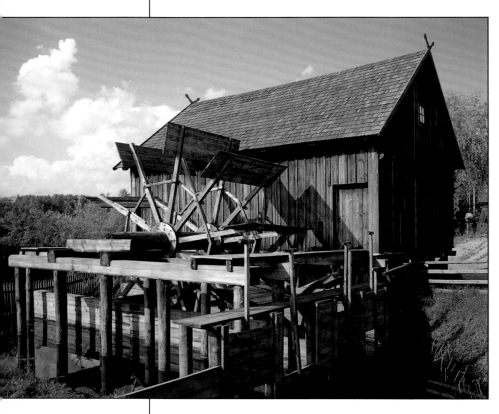

*Nowogród.
Museum of the
Kurpie Region,
the skansen
of wooden
architecture*

Admirers of old architecture, especially post-modernists bored with modern designs, will like the small town of Tykocin. Picturesquely situated on the River Narew far from the main roads, it is said to be a sleepy place where dogs are too lazy to bark and cats sleep on window sills instead of straying. The Baroque Church and Monastery of the Missionaries, the beautifully restored synagogue and

*Szczuczyn,
a post-Piarist
monastic com-
plex. Interior of
the Baroque
church*

The Biebrza marshes. The Biebrza National Park, a unique natural reserve in Europe

71

Ciechanowiec. Skansen museum of wooden folk architecture

Zuzela, the birthplace of Cardinal Stefan Wyszyński, Primate of Poland till 1981. A classroom in the former school

the 17th-century, probably first almshouse for disabled soldiers in Poland create an olden times aura around Tykocin. Time seems to have stopped here.

Apart from Białystok, two other smaller cities, Siedlce and Łomża, aspire to becoming the main cities of the Podlasie region.

Siedlce belonged to the famous aristocratic Czartoryski family. They built a neoclassical palace, later passed to another great family, the Ogińskis. Two fine parks: a landscape and a geometric one have survived from the aristocratic times. And that is all - too little for an important town.

Łomża, beautifully situated on the high Narew escarpment, looks more interesting. It used to be one of the major towns in Mazovia. It was a bishop's seat, with a late-Gothic ca-thedral, later rebuilt in the Baroque style. Huge fortifications dating from the tsarist times are a great attraction for military architecture fans.

The marshland along the Narew, which spreads for some fifty miles, is a bird sanctuary and has recently become a national park.

Hodyszewo,
a sanctuary of Our
Lady of Reconcili-
ation. Village
cemetery

*Warsaw.
Neoclassical
Palace on the
Water in Łazienki
Park*

MAZOVIA,
THE LAND OF
CHOPIN

Warsaw - the Old Town, nearly completely destroyed during the Second World War and reconstructed with great care. View of Castle Square and the statue of the Old Town Mermaid

Warsaw's coat of arms depicts a mermaid - a half-beautiful woman, half-fish. The hybrid raises her sword to some enemy. It is a suitable emblem for a city called 'Invincible'. Warsaw (Warszawa) is rather ugly, with some beautiful places; a hybrid which has always been very rebellious.

Its ugliness is an effect of the conglomeration of districts completely unmatched with one another. The city lacks any imposing structures except for the Palace of Culture and Science, built for Warsaw by Stalin's order as a gift from the 'fraternal Soviet nation'. This massive tower block in the very centre of the city, a replica of its many Moscow prototypes, would provoke many jokes and cause general disgust. Varsovians call it 'the dream of a drunk confectioner', as the construction resembles a gigantic wedding cake.

Warsaw was destroyed almost every century. In the 17th century the town was ruined by the Swedish invasion, known as 'the Deluge'. The Russian General Suvorov perpetrated a massacre of the Praga district on the right bank of the Vistula at the end of the 18th century. The town suffered from the Russians under

Warsaw –
the Royal Castle.
Monumental
elevation facing
the Vistula

Warsaw - the reconstructed interiors of the Royal Castle: Knights' Room with large-scale paintings by Bacciarelli, Ballroom and Senators' Hall with an authentic royal chair

General Paskevitch when they crushed the November Insurrection in 1831. The First World War did not inflict serious damage on Warsaw, but the Second World War nearly wiped out the city with four waves of destruction. The disaster started in September 1939, when Warsaw defended itself from the Nazi forces in complete isolation for three weeks. Then in 1943 the Germans put down the desperate Jewish Ghetto Uprising and completely erased their entire district. Then came the main Polish uprising in August and September 1944, known as the Warsaw Uprising, but the final destruction did not come until after the almost complete evacuation of the main, left bank and Hitler's insane order that no trace of the city should remain.

When the Soviet Army entered Warsaw to secure power for the communists, the city practically did not exist. It was even planned to transfer the capital to Łódź. But the overwhelming feeling was that only Warsaw, a symbol of patriotism and bravery, could be the capital of Poland. So the reconstruction of the historic district of the Old Town and the Royal Way was started and it soon yielded results.

The old quarters were brought back to their original, or even greater splendour. As most of the blueprints were lost during the war, the designers and builders had to use old photographs and even the paintings of Bernardo Bellotto, called Canaletto, a great 18th-century painter of Warsaw views. In a few years patina

Warsaw - the Old Town, included in the UNESCO World Heritage List. Old Town Market Square

Warsaw - the city centre. The Palace of Culture and Science, a controversial tower block, and the Blue Skyscraper in Bankowy Square

covered the Old Town houses and nobody in Warsaw cares that they are only half a century old.

The later decades brought pseudo-modern methods of building, such as large-panel construction. Huge, dull and featureless housing developments of blocks of flats were built in the outskirts of Warsaw, like in many other cities in Europe.

Nevertheless, some fragments of Warsaw could well belong to the most elegant of cities. Take for instance Krakowskie Przedmieście. The wide, artistically irregular street starts from Zamkowy (Castle) Square, where the soaring Sigismund III Vasa Column, another symbol of Warsaw, commemorates the ruler who transferred the capital from Cracow to Warsaw four centuries ago. Krakowskie Przedmieście is lined with mostly neoclassical but also some Baroque palaces and almost exclusively Baroque churches. Starting from the monument of the king who 'moved the capital', passing the renovated Presidential Palace and the University campus, the street ends at the monument of the

80

*Warsaw –
Łazienki Park.
Frédéric Chopin
Monument,
where Sunday
concerts of
Chopin's music
are given in
summer*

*Warsaw –
Wilanów Palace.
Façade of the
most precious
royal residence in
Poland*

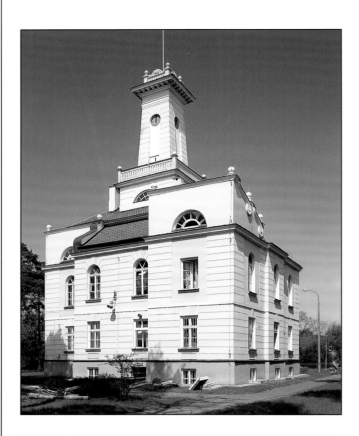

astronomer who 'moved the Earth' - Nicolaus Copernicus. Krakowskie Przedmieście passes into the gently curving Nowy Świat.

Apart from the route known as the Royal Way, linking the early-Baroque Royal Castle with neoclassical Belvedere, Warsaw has very few imposing buildings. There is the Grand Theatre, a masterpiece of neoclassicism designed by Antonio Corazzi, some fine churches, and of course the Old Town Market Square with the streets around it. Each of its houses, once owned by the Warsaw patricians, is charming, and each differs from the rest. The Gothic intermingles with the Renaissance and the Baroque, history with legend. The monster which inhabited the cellars of the Basilisk House killed people with its stare until it was approached with a mirror and killed itself. Each house has a name, e.g. The Crocodile or Baryczka, and each of them is connected with some memory. Here the shoe-maker Jan Kiliński prepared his rebellion, while

*Mińsk
Mazowiecki,
a town on the site
of a medieval
trade settlement.
17th-c. church*

82

over there lived Maria Skłodowska-Curie. Another one houses the Museum of Literature dedicated to Adam Mickiewicz (who never even visited Warsaw). Still another - the Historical Museum of Warsaw. Next to it the Fukier wine cellar, where it has been hard to find a vacant place for three hundred years.

It is impossible to list all museums, but the National Museum, situated up the Vistula escarpment off the Royal Way, is of prime importance. It has a splendid gallery of Polish painting and rich collections of foreign art.

Warsaw has some nice parks, including one on a European scale: Łazienki Park. It was designed in English style with some French elements, like the section around the Chopin Monument with a weeping willow over it. The park, arranged on a steep slope of the escarpment, is characterized by magnificent old trees, dense shrubs and a chain of ponds. A number of fine buildings gracefully complement the

Goźlin, a village in the middle Vistula valley. Interior of the wooden Baroque church

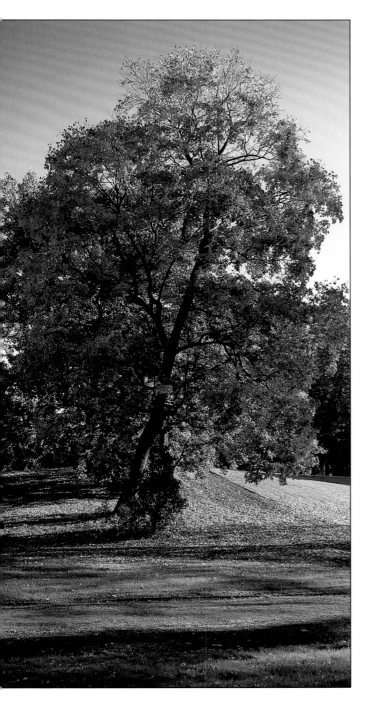

natural landscape. The Palace on the Water, a favourite residence of the last Polish king, Stanisław Augustus Poniatowski, is a perfect combination of Baroque and neoclassicism, known as the 'King Stanisław style'. The design was made by the famous architect Domenico Merlini according to the king's own ideas. The Old Orangery used to house one of the oldest theatres in Europe. The Summer Theatre on the Island is a replica of an ancient amphitheatre. A lot of other buildings are hidden amid the greenery. When feeling tired, a visitor may rest on a bench and enjoy the company of friendly park squirrels.

Jabłonna near Warsaw. Baroque-neoclassical palace and a fragment of the park

Zegrze, Serock and Nieporęt on the artificial Lake Zegrzyńskie - holiday centres with water sport facilities for Varsovians

Some insist, however, that the Ignacy Paderewski(or Skaryszew) Park in Praga district is even more beautiful than Łazienki. The English park, ornamented with hills, clusters of old trees, ponds and lush meadows, is a green oasis in the middle of a busy city.

As to the old districts of Warsaw, they must have once been very beautiful, which is reflected by the names of those former aristocratic quarters. Since in old times all fashions came from Paris, the names were derived from French. The present Mokotów has originated from Mon Coteau, that is 'my hill', as the oldest part of the district stretched over the Warsaw escarpment. Marymont is the French for Mount of Mary. Żoliborz, before the last war a district of army officers and rich intelligentsia, has been coined from Joli bord, or 'beautiful bank' (of the Vistula). The river has in the meantime moved away from Żoliborz, leaving a wide stretch of meadows, good for walking along or horse riding.The Baroque palace-cum-garden complex at Wilanów, former village, now within the city limits, is certainly worth a visit. Here

*Pułtusk
on the Narew,
former seat of the
Bishops of Płock.
Town Hall in the
market square
with the 16th-c.
tower and the
Bishops' Palace,
now Polonia
House, in the
background*

*The Mazovian
Plain with its
typical flat land-
scape*

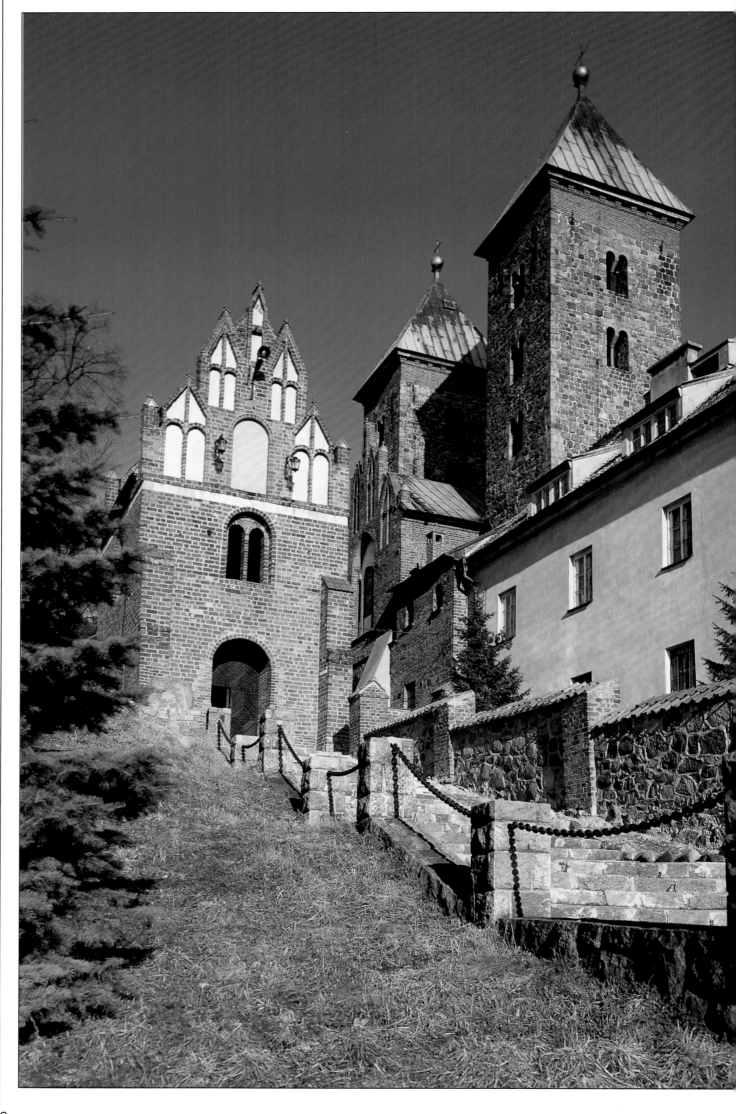

Czerwińsk on the Vistula, the former river trade centre. The former monastery of canons regular with the Romanesque Parish Church

King John III Sobieski resided with his beloved Queen Marie-Casimire, in Polish just Marysieńka. Today Wilanów is a branch of the National Museum. From time to time a royal visitor to Poland happens to reside in the palace.

At the other end of the outskirts of Warsaw stretches the Kampinos Forest, 225 square kilometres of which constitute the Kampinos National Park. It is rare that such a splendid, natural forest habitat is found so close to a great metropolis.

Outside the north edge of the Kampinos Forest, the widely flowing Vistula is joined by its largest tributaries, the Bug and Narew. These two rivers are treated as one, because geographers are unable to decide which of them flows into the other. The Bug is evidently longer, for it starts as far away as Ukraine, while the Narew

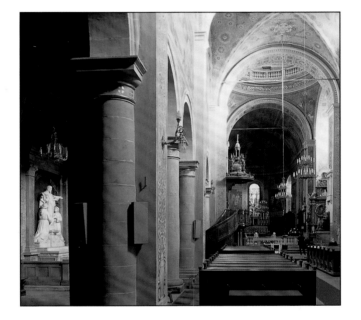

carries more water, gathered in the Podlasie and the Masuria regions.

Anyway, the Vistula swells when they join it at the foot of the Modlin fortress, built and extended from the time of Napoleon Bonaparte till the Second World War. In 1939 the defenders of Modlin continued to fight till the very end in support of besieged Warsaw.

Going down the river we arrive at Zakroczym, a town dating back to the Piast times. In 1831 it served for a week as a provisional capital of Poland, for when the November Insurrection had fallen, an army of thirty-thousand under General Maciej Rybiński still stationed

*Płock,
one of the oldest
settlements
in Mazovia, dating
back to the 10th c.
The rebuilt
Romanesque
Cathedral on
Tumskie Hill
and its interior*

*The Vistula,
Europe's last
unregulated big
river*

Żelazowa Wola, the birthplace of Frédérick Chopin. The Chopin museum

Folk costume from the Łowicz region, typical for Mazovia

vived, where Bishop Albert of Paris settled a group of French monks. This points to the fact that travel between Poland and France was not only one-way. Inside the church, some Romanesque wall paintings were uncovered. They document the early stage of development of French painting: the saints have big heads with circular halos round them and wings resembling Indian headdress. The paintings are considered by art historians to be extremely precious.

At this spot the great army of King Władysław Jagiełło crossed the Vistula on its way to Grunwald. The soldiers built a half-kilometre long bridge over the river supported on boats. It was a wonder of medieval military engineering. The Teutonic Knights' commander refused to believe his own scouts reporting that the Poles 'built a bridge in the air', and he did not bother to concentrate all his units. As a result, he lost his life and the whole of his army.

Not far from Czerwińsk is another wonder of civil engineering: the longest wooden bridge in Europe, or maybe in the whole world, at Wyszogród. It has 60 spans and 1250 metres. Every few years, when the water in the spring gets dangerously high and carries huge ice-floes, the whole country is alarmed if the bridge will withstand the pressure this time. But somehow it is always saved by brave sappers.

There are some picturesque islands on the Vistula beyond Wyszogród. Apart from providing breeding sites for seagulls, terns and other birds, including some rare species, they serve as pastures for cattle.

On the right, high bank of the Vistula emerges the beautiful skyline of Płock. Most of the historic relics in Płock lie on Tumskie Hill: the 12th-century Cathedral with soaring towers, fragments of a medieval castle and the

at Zakroczym. From here they marched to Prussia and then to France, to the 'Great Emigration'. Today Zakroczym is known as the capital of the greatest onion farming region in Poland.

At Czerwińsk, further down the Vistula, the 12th-century monastery church has sur-

Arkadia, the romantic landscape park

former Benedictine Abbey. Today Płock is the centre of the Polish petrochemical industry.

The environs of Warsaw are not particularly attractive. They are as flat as a pancake and built up with ugly suburbia. It must have looked different in the past, when young Frédéric Chopin fell in love with the idyllic Mazovian countryside. The composer's heart rests in an urn fixed into the wall of the Holy Cross Church in Warsaw, though his grave is in the Pere Lachaise cemetery in Paris.

Chopin was born in a small manor-house at Żelazowa Wola near Warsaw. It has survived and now it houses a museum devoted to the composer. Concerts of Chopin's music are performed there regularly, to the great applause of music lovers from various countries.

A little further away from Warsaw stands the imposing Nieborów Palace, designed also by Tylman van Gameren. It was the residence of Primate Radziejowski, then of the Ogiński family and finally - the famous Polish-Lithuanian family of the Radziwiłłs.

Nearby Łowicz is famous for the most beautiful folk costumes. They are still worn by the Łowicz women on such occasions as the Corpus Christi procession. This colourful event always attracts thousands of tourists.

Nieborów Palace, containing the painting gallery and sculpture collection, including ancient pieces, founded in the 18th c.

Łódź,
a city which grew
with the develop-
ment of textile
industry in the
mid-19th c.
Poznański Palace
with its rich
eclectic façade

POLISH
MANCHESTER

Łódź. Piotrkowska Street – the largest surviving complex of Art Nouveau architecture in Poland and old spinning mills

The Sieradz-Łęczyca land merges with the Łódź region, which has developed over the last two centuries. Before, there was no such region, though the little village of Łodzia

came into being during the 14th century. It was even granted a town charter in 1423, but hardly anyone had heard about it in Poland until the 19th century. In 1820 it had only 767 inhabitants and after a few decades - five hundred times more. Łódź not only emerged rapidly, but it soon became the second-biggest city in Poland, its population now amounting to one million.

A major causal factor was the invention of mechanical, initially steam-driven spinning and weaving. The first factory in Łódź, today housing the Textile Industry Museum, was built by a Mr Ludwik Geyer in 1835-7. Other businessmen followed his example and in a short time Łódź was labelled a 'Polish Manchester'. The 19th-century producers took advantage of the absence of a customs border between the Russian Empire and its partition zone called the Kingdom of Poland and they sold their fabrics to the entire tsarist empire as far as the Pacific.

Polish capitalism - or rather Polish, immigrant German, Russian and Jewish - developed in Łódź. For many decades it was

Łódź.
Modern city
centre

a cosmopolitan and rich city; rich but un-sightly. It was built up chaotically, shabbily and too densely. No attention was paid to aesthetics or basic conveniences. Łódź has been undergoing renovation for fifty years now, but it is still a gloomy city, even though the infrastructure has been greatly improved.

Obviously, you would not expect to find any historic sights in a city like this. But what

has not so far been regarded as a historic place may become it one day. This is going to happen to Piotrkowska Street. The unique, extremely long thoroughfare is lined with Art Nouveau houses. Some of the palaces in which the first tycoons resided, fenced off with high walls from unpleasant factory and workers' quarters, have now gained the status of historic monuments. As the *fin de siècle* is again in fashion, more and more people in Łódź are finding their city beautiful.

Łódź -
Radogoszcz.
Monument
mausoleum,
Museum of the
Independence
Tradition

93

*Pabianice,
a centre of the
textile industry.
Zamkowa Street
with 19th-c.
houses*

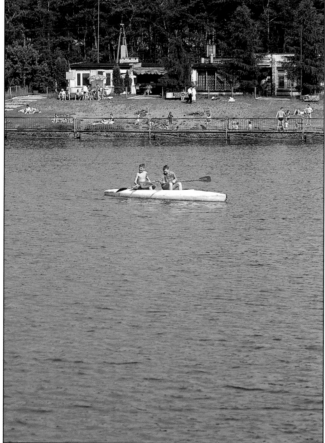

*Konstantynów
Łódzki,
a former factory
settlement,
a place for
weekend trips of
Łódź inhabitants*

The cultural circles in Łódź can take pride in at least two of the city's institutions: the Museum of Modern Art, boasting the richest collection of avant-garde painting in Poland, and the only Polish Higher School of Cinema, Theatre and TV. It was from this school that the world famous 'Polish film school' emerged in the 1950s and 1960s. Such great artists as Andrzej Wajda, Andrzej Munk, Wojciech Has, Krzysztof Zanussi, Roman Polański and Krzysztof Kieślowski made their films in the Łódź film company.

Piotrków Trybunalski, a close neighbour of Łódź, was famous before anyone had heard a word about Łódź. It was first mentioned in written records in 1217. The Gothic Parish Church and the Dominican Monastery date back to the 14th century. Many other sacred and secular buildings were erected in the Renaissance and Baroque periods, when the nobility gathered in the town for general and provincial assemblies. For nearly three centuries until the partitions of Poland Piotrków

*Zgierz,
a centre of the
textile industry.
View of the
church from the
early 20th-c.*

Skierniewice, 19th-c. railway junction on the Warsaw-Vienna line. 18th-c. Palace of Gniezno Archbishops with its neoclassical façade

Radziejowice. 17th-c. palace connected with a small castle, rebuilt in the 19th c.

was a seat of the Crown Tribunal, which settled the disputes from Mazovia and Great Poland. Piotrków inhabitants are very proud of their past and they are sorry now that their town is becoming a satellite of the nearby Bełchatów. No one knew Bełchatów until brown coal started to be extracted here. Miners have already dug a huge hollow in the ground - certainly the largest in Poland - and are making it larger and larger. The coal is used to produce electricity supply for one-fifth of Poland.

The 'greater Łódź' area is surrounded by a number of small towns with developed textile industry, such as Zduńska Wola, Zgierz, Pabianice, Aleksandrów and others. They have not much to offer to tourists, but on the other hand... At Pabianice there are

Żyrardów. Art Nouveau palace, now the Regional Museum

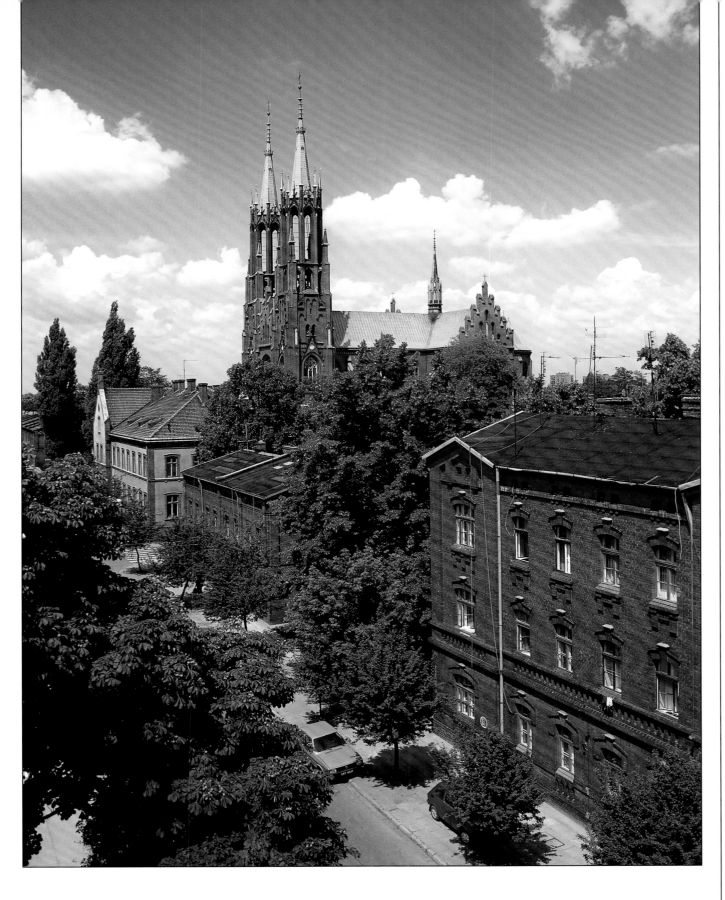

*Żyrardów,
a 19th-c. factory
settlement, a
centre of textile
industry and the
site of the first
great workers'
strike in Poland
in 1883. View
of the town*

a few traces of the Renaissance style and some old wooden houses from the early 19th century. In the Blue Springs nature reserve near Tomaszów Mazowiecki karst springs flow out profusely. Skierniewice has the famous Institute of Fruit-growing, where new and tasty apple varieties are being grown. Halfway between Łódź and Warsaw, at Radziejowice, the former Radziejowski, then Krasiński Palace today serves as a creative work centre for artists, writers and scientists. It is also a favourite place for the secret meetings of freemasons.

KALISZ
WAS KNOWN
TO PTOLEMY

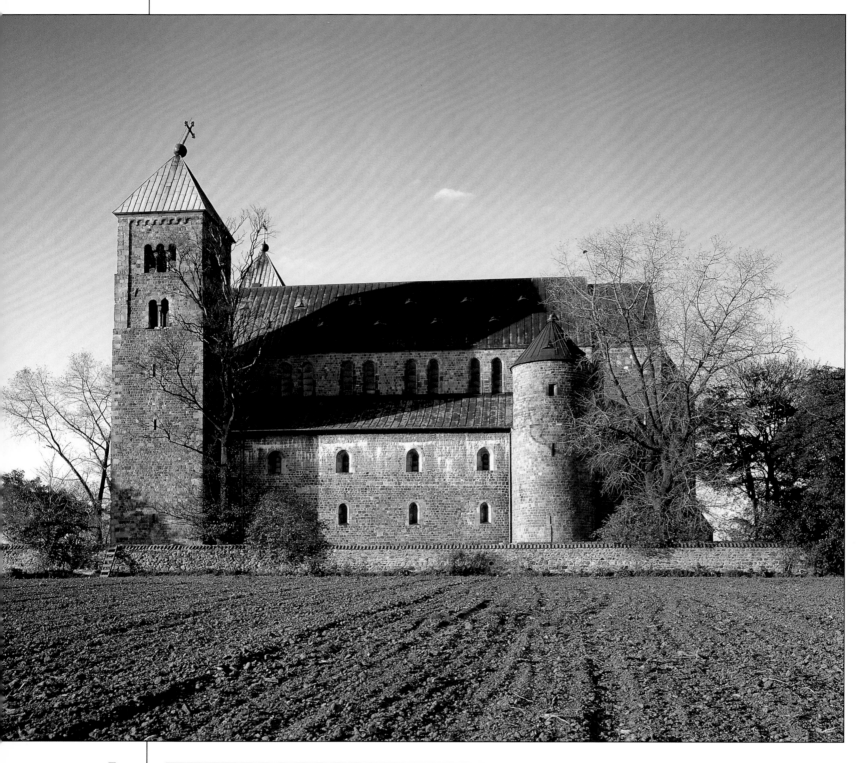

Tum near Łęczyca. 12th-c. Romanesque Collegiate Church and its severe interior

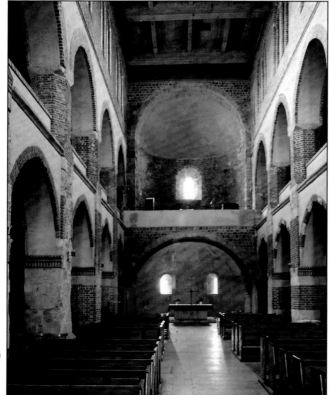

Most of the oldest towns in Poland were founded about a thousand years ago, when the Polish state was formed by the Piasts. According to archaeological studies, there were some exceptions founded much earlier.

Kalisz is an exception among exceptions. It was mentioned as 'Kalisia' (not 'Calisia' as many historians report) by Ptolemy of Alexandria himself in the 2nd century A.D. Kalisia was one of 8,000 localities on the map of the world included in his work on geographical learning, which was not available to Europeans until the 15th century, when it was already out-of-date.

The name 'Kalisia' was recorded at the time when the Roman empire was threatened by Germanic tribes and the Parthians. It became necessary to watch the barbarian lands across the Danube and the Rhine more closely. What that 'Kalisia' actually was is not clear. That it was a camp or a station of the Roman legions sounds improbable. It might have been an open trade settlement on the old Amber Route. But it cannot be ruled out that it was the centre of a small tribe of Kalisians mentioned as 'Helisians' by Tacitus even earlier than Ptolemy.

Unfortunately, archaeologists have not found any traces of that ancient Kalisia at Kalisz. The findings date back to no earlier

Łęczyca, a supposed devil's headquarters. Tower of the renovated 14th-c. castle and sculptures of devils in the castle courtyard

Koło. Ruins of the 14th-c. castle of King Casimir the Great

101

Konin, a centre of brown coal mining. Neoclassical Town Hall and a Romanesque cross in the wall of the Gothic Parish Church

Słupca. 16th-c. wooden church

The Konin region. Potato harvest

than the 9th century. One of them is the oldest beehive excavated in Poland. It has been preserved together with a honeycomb, one of those which made our forefathers' lives sweet.

At the beginning of the second millennium Kalisz developed into the seat of a little provincial duchy. Many buildings have survived from that and later times - from the Gothic to the neoclassical period. They add a patina to the town, a rather dignified and old-fashioned look. Otherwise Kalisz has no particularly valuable historic relics. The greatest damages were inflicted on old Kalisz architecture at the beginning of the First, not during the Second World War, like in most other Polish towns.

The highly valuable historic building is the mid-12th century Romanesque Collegiate Church at Tum. The village was once the central part of Łęczyca, numbered among the oldest towns in Poland, the first settlement there dating to the 6th century. Art historians find many analogies between the Tum church and the Romanesque religious architecture in Rhineland, Lorraine and even Normandy.

The Łęczyca and the neighbouring Sieradz lands lie in the very centre of Poland,

Licheń Stary, a goal of pilgrimages to the local church-sanctuary. Roman Catholic church dignitaries celebrating St. Mary's Assumption; view of the sanctuary and the church interior

*Picture
of Our Lady
of Licheń*

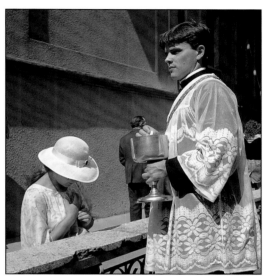

*Licheń Stary.
Confession and
Holy Communion
during the church
fete and Golgotha
Hill built of stones*

A village in the
Sieradz
voivodship.
An old thatched
cottage.

where the three historic regions of Great Poland, Mazovia and Little Poland meet. The region should be of interest for those who pursue linguistic studies on the Polish lan-

Sieradz.
15th-c. figure of
Madonna with
Child in
the Ursuline
Convent

guage. Local country people speak almost a literary language, with very little dialectic traits. Other specialists who may like this region are probably... demonologists. The most famous of Polish devils, called Boruta, Rokita and some other local names, prowled in the area. He was imagined as an elegant nobleman in traditional attire, although what he liked best was roaming the forests and swamps.

Sieradz, a town on the Warta as old as Łęczyca, was described by the 12th-century Arab geographer al-Idrisi as one of the biggest towns in Poland. A Piast duke resided here and important political rallies of the nobility took place, as well as synods of bishops. No imposing munuments of architecture are found in Sieradz beside the Dominican monastery and church from the 13th century. Instead, the cultural folk heritage of the region - much revered and still alive in some villages - has been preserved in the *skansen* of the Ethnographic Park.

North of Kalisz, halfway to Kruszwica on the ancient trail known as the Roman Amber Route, near the town of Konin, you will find a stone pillar, which is hardly ever noticed though it is probably one of the oldest preserved proto-Slavic or maybe even

Celtic figural sculptures. Whether it represented a monk or a bear cannot be told now that time has blurred its contours. When no longer needed - for its loss of quality or the people's change of faith - around the 12th century it was turned into a road post. And so it stands.

Strońsko.
Tympanum
of the early 13th-c.
Romanesque
church

Sieradz,
a town in the
picturesque Warta
Valley. Market
square

Wieluń.
Museum of the
Wieluń region in
the 17th-c. post-
Bernardine
Monastery

Is there anyone who still cares about some old piece of stone when a new vibrant industrial centre is developing around, based on brown coal extracted for the local power plant from several opencast mines in the vicinity. The cooling water from the plant is poured out very hot into the nearby lakes. As a result, some stenothermal fish species which have never before occurred in Poland appeared in these lakes.

Popowice.
16th-c. wooden
church with
shingle roof

North of Konin beyond the Grąblin forest, the towers of St. Mary's Sanctuary are seen from a distance in the village of Stary Licheń.

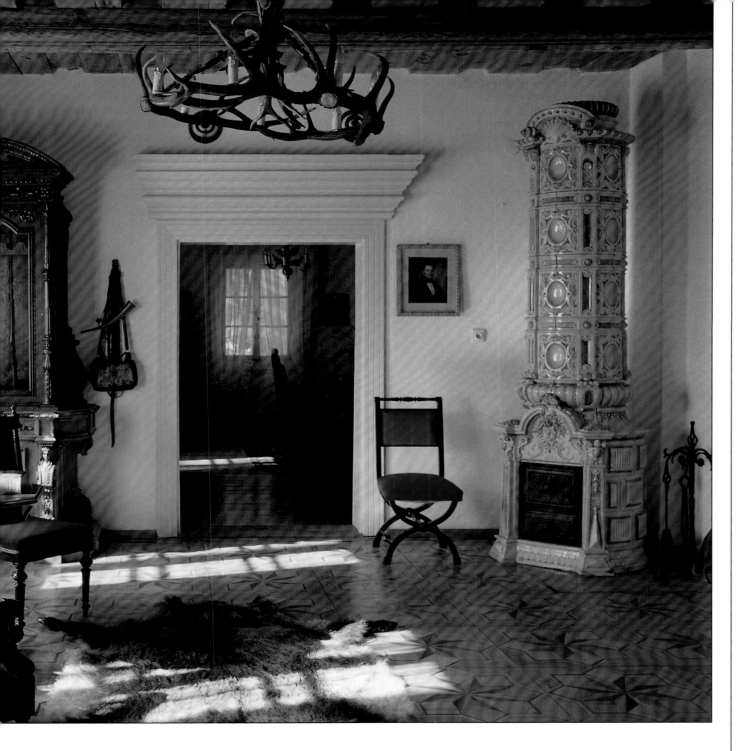

*Ożarów –
Baroque manor-
house. Museum
of Manor Interi-
ors, Hunters'
Room*

The holy site is visited by hundreds of thousands of tourists. A man-made hill called
Golgotha is quite a unique sight.

Poznań
on the Warta,
a capital of historic
Wielkopolska
region. Ostrów
Tumski with the
Cathedral dating
back to the 10th c.

THE CRADLE OF POLES

*Biskupin.
Reconstruction
of the ancient
settlement from
the Lusatian
culture*

*Gniezno,
the main castle-
town of the
Polanes in the
8th c. Fragment
of the Cathedral
and Tumska
Street*

The species of *Homo sapiens* arrived relatively late in the Polish lands, discouraged for thousands of years by severe climatic conditions. It was cold here during the four successive glacial periods, the last of which ended some 10,000 years ago. Only then did the warmer Holocene, or the present epoch start.

It was therefore a long time before any man appeared in this land or left any definite traces. If he had made some attempts to settle in Poland before the last glaciation, it must have been somewhere in the south of the country at the mountain foothills. It was not until some 8,000 years B.C. that fine forests started to grow all over Poland and palaeolithic man arrived with his quarry stone tools. He knew how to make a bow and could hunt for reindeer. He preferred to settle near water, and thus he kept advancing towards the neolithic era. When it came, he replaced his flaked stone tools with ground stone ones. He bred goats, pigs and cattle and sowed various crops, becoming more and more civilized.

Where he came from is not certain. Perhaps from the Danube. Years, centuries and millennia passed. The inhabitants of the present Poland, or - to be precise - its part called Great Poland (Wielkopolska), already believed in the afterlife and built sizeable mounds (some of them longer than a hundred metres) to their deceased. As fashions in pottery changed, clay pots were shaped into funnel beakers or spherical amphorae, then string- or stroke-ornamented and the like. The people probably spoke proto-Indo-European, from which many names have survived, such as the rivers Wisła (Vistula) and Odra (Oder).

Step by step, the Lusatian culture developed. Among a great number of its relics, the best known is the fortified settlement of Biskupin. It had 13 parallel streets encircled

Poznań.
Old Market
Square with
the Renaissance
Town Hall and
a small sculpture
of a female settler
from Bamberg

113

*Ostrów Lednicki
- the skansen
museum of
Wielkopolska
villages*

*Lake
Wieleńskie,
one of a number
of lakes dotting
the Wielkopol-
ska landscape*

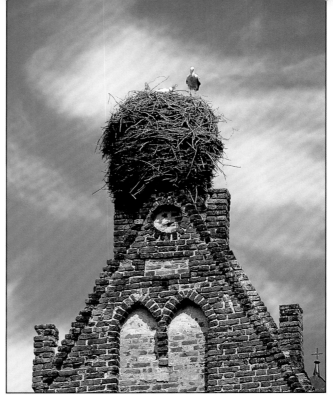

Boszkowo,
a holiday resort;
Lake Dominickie

Dębowa Łęka.
Stork's nest,
a common sight
in Poland

by a rampart with a palisade and was inhabited by around 1,000 people. For safety, it was built on a lake island, which has now turned into a peninsula. It all took place about twenty-five centuries ago, that is two centuries *ab urbe condita* (from the foundation of Rome). The Biskupin settlement was discovered in 1933 and it was partly reconstructed in its archaic shape as a relic from the early Iron Age.

It took over a thousand years more - stormy years, marked by many migrations of peoples through this land - before the Polish state began to develop from the tribe of Polanes.

Trzciel.
Wickerwork
is a traditional
local craft

Międzychód, a holiday resort for Poznań inhabitants. Market square houses

The first legendary ruler of the Polanes was a simple wheelwright (or a ploughman as other legends say), whose son, Siemowit, defeated Popiel the ruler of Gniezno. According to other legends, Popiel lived at Kruszwica on Lake Gopło and was finally devoured by mice. The famous Mouse Tower preserved at Kruszwica, where it is all said to have taken place, was in fact built several centuries later. Whatever, the Piast rulers Siemowit, Leszek and Siemomysł are believed to have united a few small tribes into one big tribe of Polanes, defeated their neighbours, the Goplanes, and brought Duke Mieszko I to the world. He united (or conquered) other Polish tribes, married the Bohemian Duchess Dobravka and was baptized in 966, thus advancing on the way to Europe.

Gniezno was then the capital of Poland. Before, it might have been a little island settlement on Lake Lednica, called Ostrów Lednicki, where the remains of some pre-Ro-

Choszczno on Lake Klukom amid beautiful forests. Chrobrego Street lined with birch trees; the surrounding forest

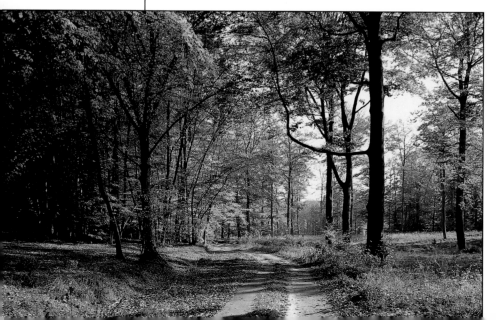

manesque stone buildings have survived, possibly among the oldest in Poland. Bolesław the Brave, son of Mieszko I and the first crowned king of Poland, liked to stay in Gniezno. His second favourite town was Poznań, where the first bishopric was established in 968. It was subordinated directly to Rome, which suggests that the 'Land of Mieszko' (the name 'Poland' came into use in later times) was from the very beginning treated as a politically independent state. Even greater favour was bestowed on Gniezno in 1000: it became an archbishops' seat. The honour of being the religious centre of Poland has been enjoyed by the town to this day.

Gniezno Cathedral, built in the Gothic style in the years 1342-72, contains an earlier, extremely valuable masterpiece of Romanesque art: the bronze doors with bas-relief, cast probably by masters from Lorraine. The doors depict the life of St. Adalbert, a Bohemian missionary to pagan Prussia killed there in 997. Relics of the saint - one of Poland's patrons - are kept in the Cathedral. The greatest statesmen of the Middle Ages, including the martyr's personal friend Emperor Otto III, came to pay respect to the relics. The Emperor presented King Bolesław with the diadem and spear of St. Maurice as a symbol of Polish sovereignty.

The present capital of Wielkopolska, Poznań, is a much bigger and more interesting town than Gniezno. The Cathedral on

Ośno Lubuskie, an old historic town. Gothic Parish Church

Gorzów Wielkopolski. Sunset on the Warta

117

*Kórnik.
Original castle
from 1426,
rebuilt
in the English
neo-Gothic style
in the 19th c. and
the Town Hall in
the market
square*

*Wschowa,
an historic town
with Baroque
buildings. Neo-
Gothic Town Hall
in the market
square and a
charming corner*

Ostrów Tumski (once an island on the Warta) was built as a pre-Romanesque basilica. In the 11th century it was extended and remodelled in the Romanesque and then in the Gothic style. Later styles - the Renaissance, Baroque and neoclassicism - also had some impact on its decoration. The Golden Chapel, the mausoleum of the Polish state founders Mieszko I and Bolesław the Brave, was re-built in the romantic Byzantine style at the beginning of the 19th century. The walls of this ancient cathedral combined nearly all styles ever flourishing in the Polish land. Alas, it was severely damaged during the fighting in 1945, and it was reconstructed in its Gothic shape, with fragments of the oldest foundations preserved in the crypt.

Poznań has many other historic buildings: the beautiful Gothic Church of the Holy Virgin Mary, with fine polychrome painting and stained glass by contemporary painter

Rydzyna, an old Baroque town. Baroque castle in a vast landscape park

Gostyń. Fragment of the Philippine monastic complex

World War, the Poznań inhabitants organized a victorious uprising against the Germans. They were the first to rebel against the Stalinist regime in 1956. Although their rebellion was suppressed with bloodshed by the communists, it initiated underground resistance in Poland. At times weaker or completely put down, the movement exploded in 1980 in Gdańsk, as the Solidarity under Lech Wałęsa. The Poznań events in 1956 also ignited the revolt in Budapest, which ended in the tragic massacre in the city by the Soviet Army.

The environs of Poznań and the whole Wielkopolska region are characterized by plain, flat landscape. The only diversity is given to it by some lakes, especially Lake Gopło, enshrouded in legend, and the forests of the Wielkopolska National Park. Local vil-

Poniec.
19th-c. Town Hall

Rawicz.
Baroque Town Hall in the market square.

Taranczewski, the Baroque Parish Church and the Town Hall, a masterpiece of the Renaissance, which could well have been transplanted from the Italian peninsula.

Compared to other Polish cities, Poznań is thought to be a reliable place with earnest and hard-working people, a wealthy city, but in the eyes of Varsovians and Cracovians a little dull and unimaginative. This maybe a false opinion resulting from the fact, that Poznań was the main city of the Prussian partition zone for over a hundred years. It may have absorbed some of the German life style, but at heart it has always remained earnestly and passionately a Polish city. When Poland was recreating itself after the First lages are famous for their economy rather than for scenic views. Still, the landscape is diversified by some magnates' palaces, now used as museums. The Baroque-neoclassical Raczyński Palace at Rogalin is known for its fine interiors, the gallery of paintings, and above all for the famous 'Rogalin oaks' of imposing size (the greatest of them is 9 me-

tres in circumference) and quantity (their number amounts to nearly one thousand). The 16th-century castle of the Działyński family at Kórnik contains historic art collections and interesting archaeological and mineral finds, also from outside Poland, as well as a library of 150,000 volumes, including many priceless old editions. The last owner of the castle, Władysław Zamoyski, offered the castle and all collections as a gift to the Polish nation. The castle park extends into a vast parkland arranged in the Italian, French and English styles from the early 19th century.

As far as sacred buildings are concerned, the early-12th-century Romanesque Collegiate Church at Kruszwica is not only very old, but also exceptionally pure in style. The rotunda of St. Procopius and Holy Trinity Church, which form part of the monastery complex of the Premonstratensian nuns at Strzelno, are not much younger. Unusually beautiful and rare Romanesque figural sculptures have been preserved inside the church.

The tradition of fairs in Poznań dates back to the 15th century. The annual Poznań International Fair was highly renowned among traders in the period between the two world wars. Since 1973 general trade fairs and industrial fairs have been held separately.

The Leszno and Lubusz lands belong to Wielkopolska, as well as the small region of Pałuki, whose rich folk culture has been preserved, and an interesting area around the towns of Śmigiel and Osieczna, where the windmills standing on hills make the landscape look like the Spanish province of La Mancha.

Góra.
Baroque interior of
the Gothic church

Klępsk.
Gothic sculptures
in the 16th-c.
wooden church

Golejewko.
19th-c. palace
amid a landscape
park

123

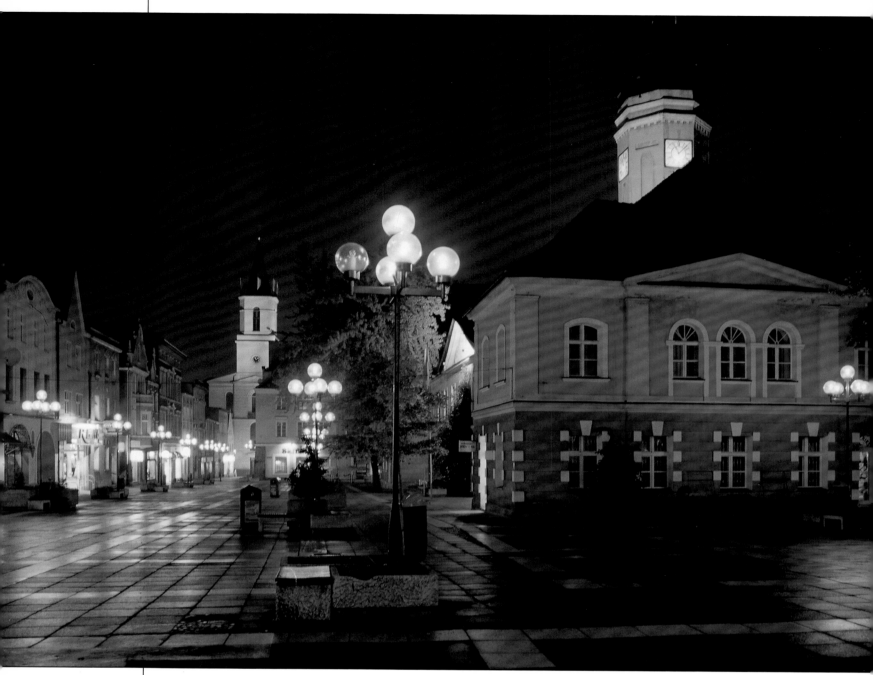

Zielona Góra, the capital of the Lubusz Land, known for its vine harvest festival. Old Market Square, the 17th-c. Town Hall and a view of the Church of Our Lady of Częstochowa

Leszno, a town bordering on the region of Silesia, was owned by the Wieniawa family, later renamed Leszczyński - prominent aristocrats. In the 16th century Leszno became a scientific, cultural and publishing centre of the Bohemian and Moravian Brethren, who escaped to Poland from persecution in their homeland. Their leader and rector of the local university was the famous pedagogue and philosopher Jan Amos Komensky, who later in his life continued his activity based on the teachings of Jan Huss in Amsterdam. Leszno has a number of precious Baroque structures, like the Town Hall finely rebuilt by Pompeo Ferrari. The Baroque castle at Rydzyna belonged to the families of Leszczyński and then Sułkowski - the founders of the once excellent Piarist Academy.

The Lubusz region, named after the frontier town now in Germany and called

Sulechów. 15th-c. Gothic Parish Church

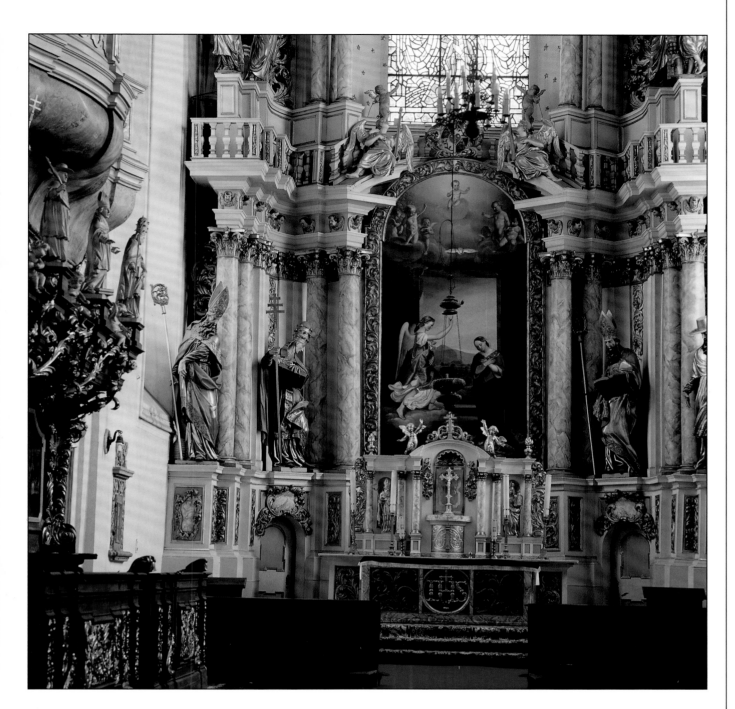

Lebus, has two rivalling cities: Zielona Góra and Gorzów. It is also characterized by much more diversified landscape full of forests and lakes. At Łagów, the beautiful 14th-century knights' castle standing on an isthmus between two lakes attracts the 'best society' of film makers, at whose events guests are treated with the local wine, made of grapes grown in the vicinity of Zielona Góra.

THE MONGOLS CAME AS FAR

Legnica was truly unfortunate. At its walls Duke Henry the Pious lost a decisive battle with the Tartar hordes in 1241. They came from the huge Mongol Empire united under Genghis Khan. When they invaded Europe, the Poles stood against them despite being divided into several dukedoms. All in vain. The prince and his best knights were killed. Nevertheless, weakened by their own losses, the Tartars decided not to proceed further to the west. Europe was saved.

Later Legnica, along with most of Silesia, was conquered by the Bohemians, then by the Habsburgs and the Prussian Hohenzollerns, Hitler's Nazis, and finally by that Genghis Khan of the 20th century - Joseph Stalin. He chose Legnica as his westernmost base and the main Soviet army quarters in Poland. Like the Mongols in the past, the stationed soldiers were prepared to attack the West.

The bad times have passed. Not a single Russian soldier stations in Poland any more. Legnica has been paid with good fortune, for it has become the centre of a dynamic copper industry. The present output amounts to 5 per cent of total world production and copper is accompanied by silver (7 per cent of world production). Silver, as we know, always comes with gold, but its output is a trade secret.

Karpacz, a holiday and tourist resort at the foot of Śnieżka. 13th-c. Wang Church brought from Norway in the 19th c.

Niedźwiedzia (Bear's) Cave in the Sudetes at the foot of the massif of Śnieżnik, the richest in Poland in dripping features

The Karkonosze, a mountain range in the Sudetes with the highest peak Śnieżka (1602 m), especially beautiful in winter

Silesia is one of the main five historic regions of Poland, along with Wielkopolska (Great Poland), Małopolska (Little Poland), Mazovia and Pomerania.

Silesia is divided into three parts. Lower Silesia borders with Germany on the River Nysa (Neisse); Upper Silesia has been the main industrial area in Poland for the last hundred years; Opole Silesia straddles the two.

The Sudetes are an attraction of Lower Silesia. These old mountains have been carved into fantastic shapes over time. There are plenty of rock cirques, winding ravines, scree slopes and strange rocky formations. The Sudetes consist of many ranges and massifs cut by deep valleys. The Karkonosze is the highest and steepest massif in the Sudetes, with the single barren peak of Śnieżka (1604 m) resembling a volcano, and otherwise a lunar landscape. A few holiday spots at the foothills of the

Karkonosze, such as Karpacz and Szklarska Poręba, are frequented by skiers, though rather by beginners. An attraction in Karpacz is the early–13th-century wooden church transferred here from Wang in Norway and reconstructed with great care.

The spacious low valley surrounded by the Kaczawskie and Sowie Mountains, contains the beautiful town of Jelenia Góra. It has some Gothic and Baroque churches, a fine old market square and some remains of medieval strongholds.

At the foothills of the Sutedes is a number of small but often interesting towns. At Kowary, an old factory continues to produce Smyrnean rugs, while the uranium mine next to it has already closed down. Chełmsko Śląskie has some charming wooden weavers' houses from the beginning of the 18th century while Krzeszów can boast a 13th-century Cistercian Abbey and

Legnica, a settlement from before the 10th c. The historic town centre spoiled by post-war architecture

one of the most beautiful late-Baroque churches in Poland. The imposing castle at Książ near Wałbrzych, built in the 16th century over much older foundations, is surrounded with 'hanging gardens' and a vast park in the English style.

The next basin encompasses Kłodzko, a stronghold on the route from Poland to the Czech lands from the 10th century. Czech influence is clearly visible in its architecture, for example in the Gothic bridge, a replica of the Charles Bridge in Prague. Tourists are fascinated by the massive fortress towering above Kłodzko built by the King of Prussia, Frederick II. Its dungeons are an object of studies and a subject for thrillers.

From Kłodzko via a chain of spas: Polanica, Duszniki Zdrój, where Frédéric Chopin gave concerts when he was 16 and now piano music festivals are held, and Kudowa we reach a peculiar part of the Sudetes - the Stołowe

Wrocław, a historic city on the Oder. Old Town Market Square with a tourist train and the Gothic Town Hall

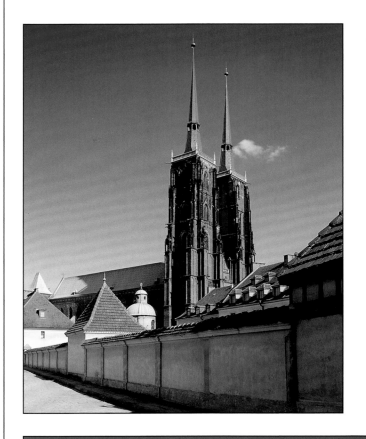

Wrocław, a settlement of the Slavic tribe of Ślężanie in the first millennium. Ostrów Tumski, St. John the Baptist's Cathedral

Opole, a town connected with Polish and German history. 19th-c. Town Hall modelled on the Palazzo Vecchio in Florence

Moszna near Opole. Eclectic castle built at the end of the 19th c.

(Table) Mountains. From a distance they seem to be nothing special, just some squat and flattened mountain ridge. A surprise lies in wait as the visitor gets closer. The upper parts are like a gigantic maze carved by erosion, where you can roam for hours on end seeing only a narrow strip of the sky above and admiring all the strange rock shapes resembling elephants, bears and eagle heads.

Many Lower Silesian towns are worthy of note. Świdnica apparently used to be called 'little Cracow'. Lubiąż has preserved the huge edifice of the Cistercian Abbey, which looks like the famous Escorial near Madrid and its cubature surpasses that of Wawel Castle in Cracow.

Wrocław, the capital of the region, is a peculiar city - both for its great past and many historic relics, including the Gothic Town Hall, and for its fascinating present. In the last months of the Second World War the city was turned

Cieszyn, a fine town on the Olza, the capital of Cieszyn (Teschen) Silesia, whose legendary beginnings date to 810. Głęboka Street with a view of the Castle and the Piast Tower; the Wooden Market Square

by the Nazis into an enormous citadel, *die Festung Breslau*. Wrocław was almost as utterly destroyed as Warsaw: 70 per cent of the houses lay in ruin. Almost all German inhabitants fled to the West or were deported after the war. Thousands of Poles from various regions settled in the city, but initially it was under the great influence of the intelligentsia from Lviw (Lvov), a city lost by Poland to the Soviet Union and now the major city of the Western Ukraine. Within a few years new Wrocław became a major Polish city after Warsaw and Cracow. The local university prospered and its school of mathematics gained high international renown. Innovative artistic trends developed. Jerzy Grotowski's Laboratory Theatre was internationally recognized as the revival of the theatre by drawing, among others, from the art of ancient India. In the 1960s Henryk Tomaszewski's pantomime theatre won similar fame.

On Ostrów Tumski island in the old city centre life is focused around the imposing 13th-century Cathedral, surrounded by several other churches and monasteries. Here reigns a serious mood, born of medieval mysticism.

It is amazing how quickly the new inhabitants of Lower Silesia can integrate, no matter where they come from. And they come from all parts of the country, often from remote villages. A lot of Poles have repatriated from the West: France, Belgium, Westphalia, Britain, Yugoslavia, Rumania or even Canada. Many Greeks and Macedonians who settled in Wrocław in the 1940s, the Ukrainians displaced from the Bieszczady Mountains and the Lemks from the Beskid Niski became wholly Polonized.

In neighbouring Opole Silesia things were a bit different. In some areas of this region the autochthonous population of German descent prevails (though before the Second World War many of them regarded themselves as Poles and were against uniting with Germany). Now they have their own German institutions, schools and unions. They delegate their own deputies to the Sejm, at the same time staying loyal to the Polish state.

Opole is a pleasant city with some old relics. The most precious of them is the 14th-century Piast Tower. Once a year this peaceful town fills with crowds of visitors from the whole country who come to attend the popular Festival of Polish Song, held in Opole for over 40 years.

The monument to Polish insurgents on St. Anne's Mountain commemorates their fierce struggle against the Germans after the First

Żywiec
at the foot of the
Beskids, known
for Żywiec beer.
A small church

Będzin.
14th-c. castle, now
the Museum of
Industrial District

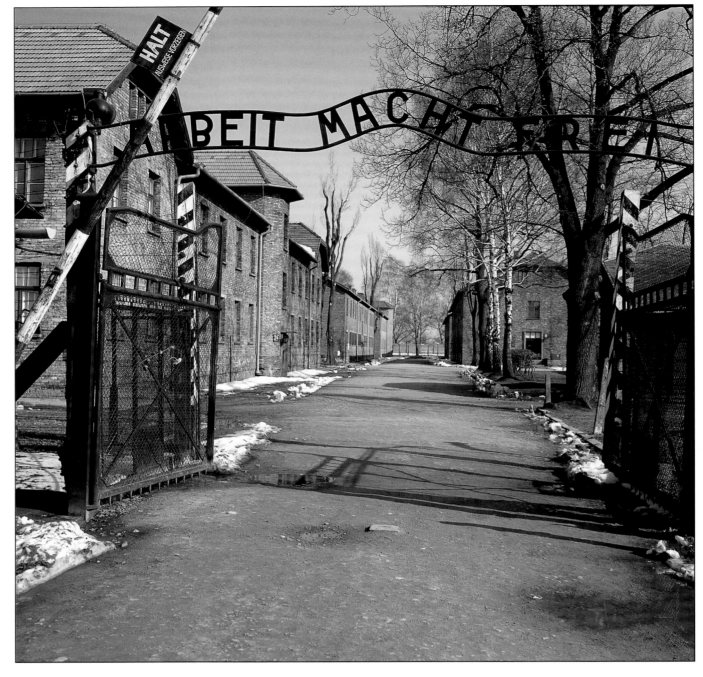

Oświęcim-Auschwitz. Museum on the site of the former Nazi concentration camp

Katowice. Imposing Monument to Silesian Insurgents in front of the Spodek (Saucer) show and sportshall and a historic building in the city centre

World War. Today the monument is treated as a symbol of Polish and German reconciliation and mutual forgiveness of the harms inflicted.

In the east the Opole region merges with Upper Silesia, where in poet Julian Tuwim's words, 'Coal and steel have their say'.

In Upper Silesia the earth is black and ill with fatigue. Only men of business come here. Others would rather exclude the main Upper Silesian cities - Katowice, Chorzów, Zabrze, Bytom, Gliwice, as well as many smaller towns - from their itinerary, although there are quite

a number of interesting sights in the area.

Only the southern edge of Upper Silesia - the mountains and their foothills - is free from fumes, noise and other kinds of pollution. The Beskids offer good and very popular skiing facilities in the villages of Szczyrk, Wisła and Korbielowa. At Koniaków and Istebna the enchanting folklore of the Beskid highlanders is still blooming. The nearby old Cieszyn, divided

into the Polish and the Czech part by the River Olza, is Poland's main gate to the South.

One place name in the region fills everyone with terror. A symbol of the Holocaust - in German Auschwitz, in Polish Oświęcim. The site of the largest Nazi death camp, where millions of victims were burnt in crematoriums. The majority of them were Jews. A visitor can only cry over their ashes.

Katowice.
Wujek coal mine,
a symbol of Polish
resistance to
martial law
imposed in 1981

Miners dressed
in special
uniforms for
celebration

*Olsztyn
near Częstochowa.
Scenic ruins of
the 14th-c. castle
set in the land-
scape of the
Cracow-
Częstochowa
Upland*

THE HEART AND SOUL OF POLES

Cracow, Wawel on a limestone hill overlooking the Vistula comprises the Gothic-Renaissance Royal Castle, Gothic Cathedral and defence walls. The castle courtyard with Renaissance cloisters; St. Stanisław's tomb in the transept of the Cathedral and Wawel Cathedral

The region we are now approaching is most difficult to describe, for it can only be praised and that may raise the reader's doubts.

Before we come to the most beautiful Polish town, let us see a real wonder, a sight unique in the world: the Wieliczka salt mine. It was the royal domain, but in 1105 King Bolesław the Wry-mouthed conferred the privilege of collecting the income from the mine to the Benedictine Abbey at Tyniec. Later, the mine was leased to wealthy families, who amassed still greater riches from it. A similar mine was built in neighbouring Bochnia. Both are still exploited, though on a smaller scale. The old parts of the mine, extending to a depth of 315 metres, have been turned into a museum, which comprises a few hundred chambers and corridors, including the famous 'crystal chambers' decorated with figures of saints carved in blocks of salt, altars, chandeliers and other ornaments.

Cracow. Main Market Square with the Cloth Hall and Mickiewicz Monument; Jewish tourists in the Kazimierz district; Lajkonik, a hobby-horse typical of the Cracow folklore

the dragon more spicy than a virgin for the monster rushed to swallow it. Immediately, the beast's stomach set on fire. To put out the flames, it descended to the water and started to drink until it drank half of the river. Then it burst. The shoemaker got his reward - the princess, and Krak set up his residence on the hill rescued from dragon.

From Wieliczka it is only a short distance to Cracow (Kraków). Tied by the neat ribbon of the River Vistula, the city boasts the most precious historic site and architectural ensemble in Poland: the castle and cathedral on Wawel Hill.

First comes the legend. Once upon a time, a terrible dragon dwelled in a cave in this hill. It would eat only the most beautiful virgins and in old times dragons had no reason to fear they would die of hunger. None of the knights of the wealthy Duke Krak was brave enough to fight with the dragon, though the promised splendid reward was marriage with the Duke's daughter. Only a simple shoemaker undertook the task. He tore the skin of a sheep, filled it with sulphur and tar and left it by the dragon's cave. The sheep must have appeared to

Some records indicate the Vislanes formed their little state a century earlier than the Polanes. According to *The life of St. Methodius*, a powerful pagan duke lived there. He refused to be baptized and 'did harm to Christians', and eventually he was baptized by force in the foreign land. It may have been the Moravian state, ruling over the upper Vistula and Cracow for several decades at the turn of the 9th century. The land was then seized by the Polanes. Gniezno and Poznań were the centres of the emerging Polish state. Around the mid-11th century Cracow grew in importance again and, as the largest town in Poland and a major European trade centre, it started to play the role of a capital. When the Polish duchies were united at the beginning of the 14th century, Cracow grew into a big and rich town, worthy of the University founded by King Casimir the Great - the second one in Central Europe after the University of Prague and older than any of the German universities.

Both the layout of that old Cracow and most of the houses within the old defence walls have been preserved. On these old walls around the Old Town a green belt was laid out

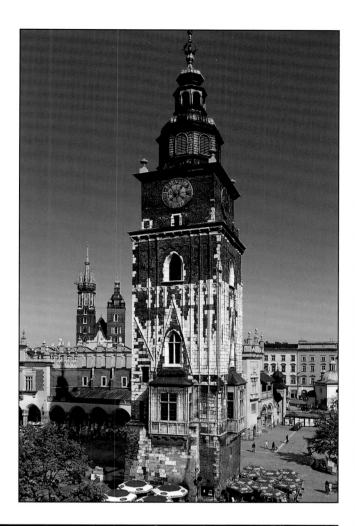

Cracow – Main Market Square. A unique view of its three towers: the Gothic Town Hall Tower and the towers of St. Mary's

Cracow – St. Mary's Church. Detail of the altar carved by Veit Stoss in lime wood in 1477-89

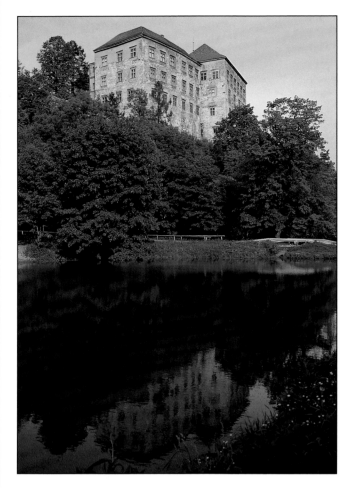

Pieskowa Skała. Gothic-Renaissance knights' castle, one of the most picturesque in Poland

The bat – a cave dweller

Ojców caves: Łokietka (Władysław the Short's) with the Knights' Chamber and Nietoperzowa (Bat Cave)

(called *Planty* i.e. Plantations), but certain fragments, such as the fine Barbican and Floriańska Gate have survived intact to this day.

The massive walls surrounding the Wawel have survived, too, together with the fine Renaissance Royal Castle and the Cathedral where Polish kings were crowned.

Wawel Castle is a museum with rich collections, such as one of the world's most valuable assemblies of wall carpets called *arrasy*. There is a gallery of oriental art and the crown treasury, where the coronation sword of Polish kings, *Szczerbiec*, is kept. The Cathedral also dates back to the pre-Romanesque and Romanesque periods, but it is mainly Gothic in style. Its aisles are surrounded by eighteen Renaissance and Baroque chapels. The Sigismund Chapel, built by Bartolommeo Berecci, is considered to be one of the greatest Renaissance buildings in Europe. The last two Jagiellons, to whom Cracow owes a great deal, rest under its gilt roof: Sigismund the Old and Sigismund Augustus. The Gothic sarcophagus of Casimir Jagiellończyk was made by Veit Stoss (in Polish Wit Stwosz), the famous sculptor of the end of the Gothic and the beginning of the Renaissance periods. Other priceless objects include King Władysław Jagiełło's favourite Byzantine-Ruthenian polychrome painting and the sarcophagus of St. Stanisław made by masters from Gdańsk in 1671. In the Cathedral treasury are housed splendid works of religious art, coronation insignia and St. Maurice's spear presented to King Bolesław the Brave by Emperor Otto III. The giant Sigismund Bell in the Ca-

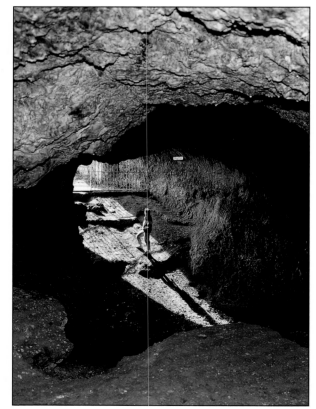

Ojców in the Prądnik Valley, a holiday and health resort since the 19th c., the centre of Ojców National Park. Castle Road

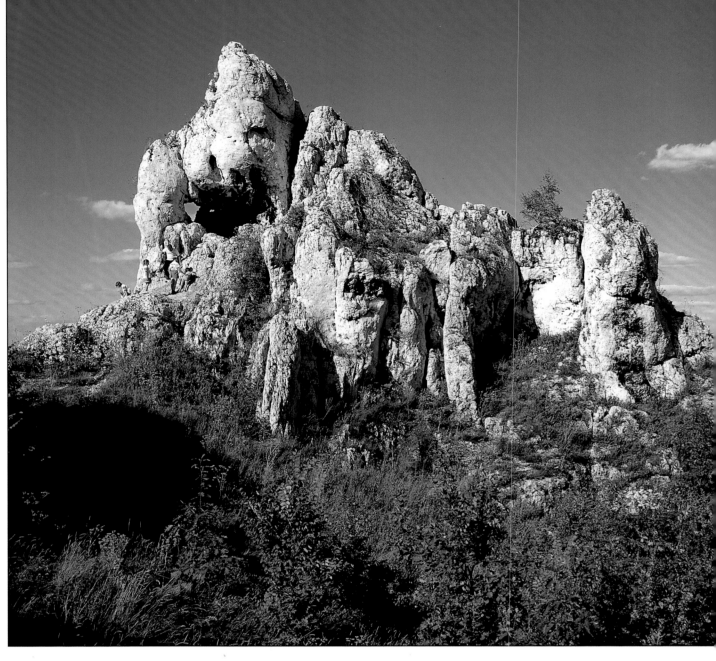

Characteristic rocks in the Cracow-Częstochowa Upland

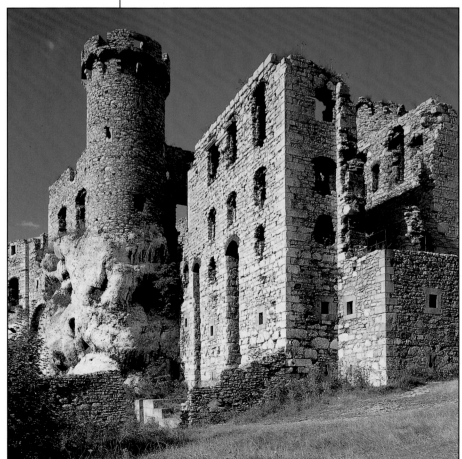

Ogrodzieniec. Ruins of the 16th-c. Renaissance fortified castle

thedral tower, eight metres in circumference, sounds only on the most special state occasions.

The most precious of all is the whole Old Town of Cracow, which has preserved its medieval urban layout. Its most important sites are the Cloth Hall - a long 14th-century market hall beautifully remodelled in the Renaissance period, the Gothic Town Hall Tower (the Town Hall building has not survived), the little Church of St. Adalbert from the end of the 11th century, and, above all, the imposing St. Mary's Church, built of brick and stone in the Gothic style with two differently finished towers. For hundreds of years a bugle-call has been sent out every hour from the higher tower and its sound always breaks in the middle. This is supposed to commemorate the 13th-century trumpeter alarming the city whose throat was pierced by an arrow shot by a Tartar soldier. The high altar of the church was carved by Veit Stoss of Nuremberg who found a second homeland in Poland. This pentaptych, 11 m wide and 13 m high, is a masterpiece of late-Gothic sculpture.

Most houses surrounding the Cracow Market Square date from the 14th to 16th centuries. In spite of later alterations, their old architecture has been largely preserved.

Lovers of painting should not miss the Czartoryski Museum in Cracow. It boasts Leonardo da Vinci's 'Lady with an Ermine', which in the opinion of many connoisseurs absolutely matches his 'Mona Lisa', and Rembrandt's 'Landscape with Good Samaritan'.

Cracow has more than a dozen churches of great historic value and a few hundred such houses. The Jagiellonian Library collections comprise unique texts from the distant past. A masterpiece of the Gothic style and the oldest part of the Jagiellonian University, the Collegium Maius, today serves as a museum of this ancient school. Among its exhibits, a 16th-

Błędowska Desert, the only desert land in Central Europe, is getting more and more overgrown

Mirów. 14th-c. castle in ruins

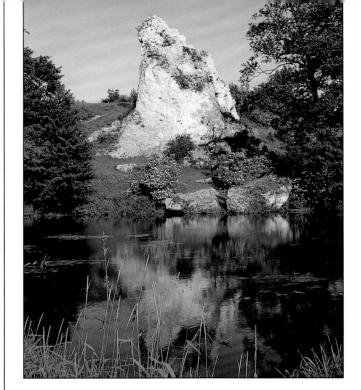

Mstów.
Miłosna (Love)
Rock on the
Warta

century globe on which America was marked for the first time in history and astronomic devices used by Nicolaus Copernicus are of particular interest.

Just a brief look at the environs of Cracow. At Bielany the towers of the Camaldolite Church and Monastery rise above the surrounding woods. On a rocky hill above the Vistula narrowing at Tyniec stand the age-old walls of the 11th-century Benedictine Abbey.

The valley of the little River Prądnik, cutting a small mountain ridge near Cracow, is extremely attractive and quite unique. The steep canyon walls are ornamented with rocks in fantastic shapes, one of which is called the Hercules' Club. This is the area of the Ojców National Park, abounding in vegetation and historic monuments. The local caves provided shelter for palaeolithic men and mammoth hunters. Legend has it that in the 13th century they were a hiding-place of King Władysław the Short, the one who strove to unite Poland in times of feudal disintegration. At Pieskowa Skała, a magnificent 14th-century Gothic-Renaissance castle stands proudly on a precipitous rock above the River Prądnik.

The Cracow-Częstochowa Upland, or Jura, a range of limestone hills destroyed by erosion and the movements of glaciers, initially rises at Ojców. The strangely-shaped island mountains known in Polish as *ostańce* are quite an attraction, and many of them contain the ruins of medieval castles; Tenczyn, Rabsztyn, Smoleń, Bobolice, Mirów, Ogrodzieniec (at

Potok Złoty,
a holiday spot.
Interior of the
Raczyński Palace
and Twardowski
Gate

Olsztyn
near
Częstochowa.
A fireworks
display

148

504 m the highest of all), Morsko and Olsztyn are but some examples.

In the west, the Jura neighbours on a Polish curiosity, which unfortunately is gradually disappearing: the Błędowska Desert. It possesses all the characteristics of a desert except camels. Mirages have been recorded. But the local dunes have been used for industrial purposes and housing spreads towards the desert outskirts.

In the north, the Jura is getting lower until it merges with the level upland and disappears amid towns and industrial plants. At its other end lies the town of Częstochowa with its treasure, Jasna Góra (Bright Mountain). Known as the 'Polish Lourdes', it is a popular sanctuary and goal of countless pilgrimages by the faithful. The darkened, beautiful Gothic chapel of the huge Pauline Monastery dating to 1382 on the mountain top contains the famous icon of the Black Madonna. This magnificent image of the Holy Virgin Mary, set on an inlaid ebony altar, has for ages drawn millions of pilgrims seeking their conciliation in the thoughtful eyes of the Madonna. When partitioned Poland suffered the slavery imposed on it by its three neighbouring powers, this image of the Virgin Mary, the patroness and Queen of the Poles, symbolically enthroned by

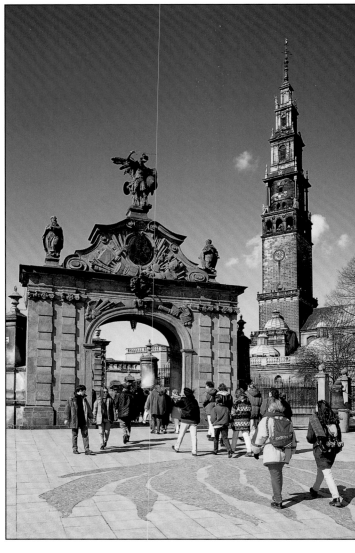

Częstochowa – Pauline Monastery on Jasna Góra, a goal of pilgrimages and a cult place of Our Lady of Częstochowa. Lubomirski Gate with the church tower; always crowded Old Town within the monastic complex; interior of the Basilica of the Ascension of the Holy Virgin Mary on Jasna Góra

150

King John Casimir in gratitude for saving the country from the Swedish 'Deluge', united all Poles and reminded them of their duties toward the enslaved but still alive Fatherland.

The region's
landscape with
wild poppies in
bloom

THE EUROPEAN FLINT TOOL CENTRE

Krzemionki, the biggest neolithic flint mine in Europe, a historic monument. Traces of holes, flint spearheads and the reconstruction of a settlement

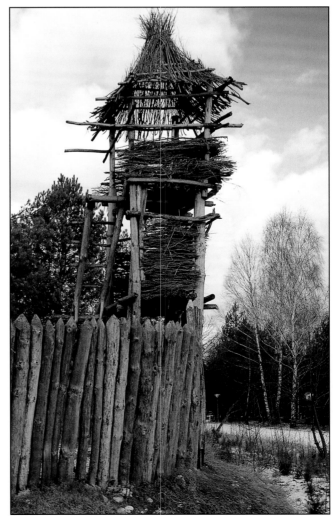

Four thousand years ago the chipped flint industry was a major branch of production. Flint is a hard stone. Flint tools were good for loosening soil and killing game - and of course enemies. The area of Krzemionki near Ostrowiec Świętokrzyski is recognized as the greatest European flint basin of the neolithic period. The raw material was dug deep in the ground and it was chipped into tools and arms on the spot.

Local axes were an export product as important as tanks today. They have been excavated from the Ukraine to the River Elbe in Germany. They are easily recognizable, for they are all marked with stripes. A large mining field of our neolithic forefathers has been preserved at Krzemionki. It had as many as 3,000 shafts, some of which were 10 to 12 metres in diameter and about the same depth. The shafts were connected by underground tunnels, which were shored up and ventilated through special holes. The ancient mine is a unique archaeological reserve and a precious prehistoric site.

Industrial activity was continued in Roman times. In the 1st and 2nd centuries A.D. the area specialized in metallurgy. Metal tools, nails, swords and spearheads were smelted, also for export.

Those industrial traditions were revived in the Kielce region a few centuries ago. Copper, silver, lead and iron ores from the Świętokrzyskie (Holy Cross) Mountains began to be extracted and processed on a greater scale. The Old Polish Industrial Centre developed around the ancient, worn-out mountains.

Today the mountains are still overgrown with the famous Fir Forest, turned into a national park,

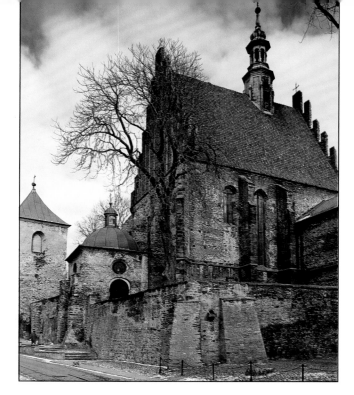

Szydłowiec. Late-Gothic church preserved in its original shape

though industrial pollution mainly from the local cement mills and lime kilns has caused a serious decline of forest. The remains of old industrial constructions from the 18th and 19th century, e.g. the metallurgical furnaces at Samsonów and the dam at Nietulisko, are protected as historic monuments. Another tourist attraction, the biggest (13.4 m in trunk diameter) and oldest oak tree in Poland, called Bartek, must remember the times of Mieszko I.

Wąchock, a flint tool centre in the Stone Age. The Cistersian Abbey

Radom. Theatre in the old building of the fire station with the monument of painter Jacek Malczewski

155

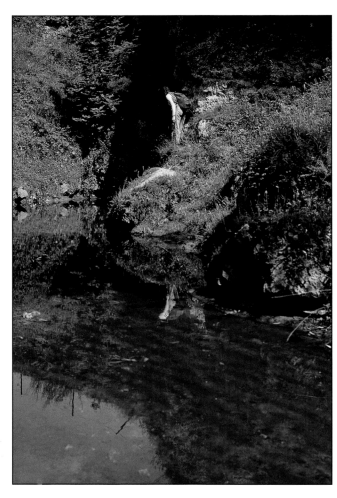

Skorocice near Busko Zdrój. Grassland reserve with karst topography, caves and tors

Chęciny. Picturesque ruins of a 13th-c. castle

The highest points of the Świętokrzyskie Mountains are Łysica (612 m), also called St. Catherine, and Łysa Góra, or Holy Cross (595 m), covered with boulder fields. In the 8th and 9th centuries a major centre of pagan cult in Poland existed on Łysa Góra. Some fragments of its walls have survived.

To bring an end to paganism, Duke Bolesław the Wry-mouthed founded the Benedictine Abbey on Łysa Góra at the onset of the 12th century. In the 19th century it was turned into an infamous prison. Today the monastic complex is administered by some tourist organizations. Next to it a 138-metre television broadcasting tower has been raised, offering a wide view of the surroundings. Some traces of pagan cults have survived in folk legends, in which Łysa Góra is described as a meeting place of witches, flying up there on broomsticks from all over the country.

Kielce, the capital of the region, existed as early as the 11th century as a trade settlement. Initially it was owned by the archbishops of Cracow, then - as a 'liberated town' - it grew into the main centre of the Old Polish Industrial Basin (the name coined by contemporary historians). Before Poland was finally partitioned, Kielce was incorporated into

Tokarnia. Ethnographic Park of the Museum of Kielce Countryside. A peasant farm, cottage interior and folk sculptures

the royal estate in 1789. Unlike its environs, the city itself has not much to offer to tourists. Only the 17th-century Bishops' Palace with early-Baroque interiors and a beautiful Baroque arcaded house in the Market Square with a museum rich in ethnographic collections remind of Kielce's past glory.

On great occasions Kielce folklore can be witnessed spontaneously in some villages. As the regional costumes are ornate and expensive, they are passed from mothers to daughters and from fathers to sons. When put on, they are quite a show.

The picturesque Baroque Benedictine Monastery on Karczówka hill near Kielce stands out from the city. In the nearby Chęciny, massive ruins of a fortified castle built by Bishop Jan Muskata have survived on a hilltop. The historic town at its foot has narrow streets lined with several hundred years' old burghers' houses and two monasteries: of the Franciscans and the Poor Clares. Fragments of streets and squares laid with fine marble from the local quarries have been preserved.

Radom is Kielce's rival town, almost equally old but completely industrialized. A lot of historic relics have survived, some of them dating back to the 14th century. However, Radom is known best for its tradition of revolutionary struggle, the workers' rebellion against the communist regime in 1976 in particular. It prompted the activity of the Committee to Defend the Workers (KOR), which already operated half-openly. Its members later became the chief leaders and consultants of Solidarity.

157

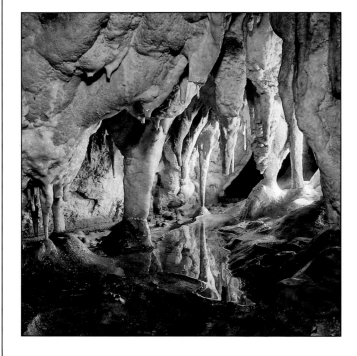

Raj (Paradise) Cave, rich in drippings and containing traces of Neanderthal man

Kadzielnia. Old quarry and a geological reserve

History dwells in the walls of castles, churches and in cemeteries of many little towns and villages of the Kielce region. At Szydłowiec, where sandstone was mined for building material as early as the Middle Ages, the 15th-century castle of the Szydłowiecki family has been preserved. It was later rebuilt by the Radziwiłłs, the famous Lithuanian-Polish aristocratic family related to some ruling dynasties in the West, into one of their countless residences. The Town Hall has retained its fine form and beautifully carved 18th-century tombstones can be seen at the historic Jewish cemetery.

At the village of Szydłów a complex of historic buildings has survived. It comprises the 14th-century castle and Parish Church with a fragment of defence walls and the fine Cracow Gate, as well as a synagogue from later times.

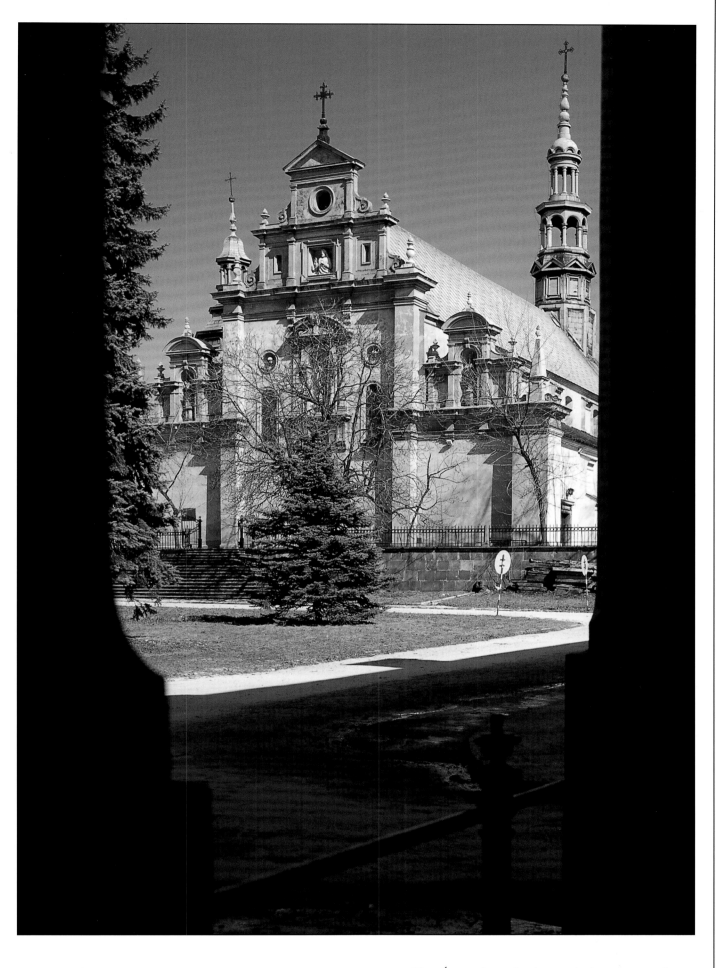

*Kielce,
a 16th-c. centre
of metal ore
mining. 17th-c.
Cathedral of the
Ascension of the
Holy Virgin Mary*

The Cistersian Abbey at Wąchock is older still. Founded in 1179, it is a good example of the transition period between the Romanesque and the Gothic styles in architecture. The Cistersian Order, a model of medieval piety and good husbandry, evidently favoured that style. The Collegiate Church at Opatów dating from the same period was extended and beautifully decorated.

The Świętokrzyski (or Kielce) region is famous for its karst caves shrouded in legends. The most beautiful and frequented Raj (Paradise) Cave near Chęciny is adorned with stalactites and stalagmites of fantastic shapes. Thus, the region offers everything a tourist looks for: traces of ancient history, natural wonders, masterpieces of architecture and rich folklore, not to mention devils and witches.

Kazimierz Dolny, a town pictur-esquely situated on the Vistula, with Renaissance town plan. Part of the town.

WHERE THE VISTULA IS MOST BEAUTIFUL

Lublin,
a fortified
settlement from
the 12th c.,
destroyed by
invaders from the
east. 14th-c. castle
ruined in the 19th
c. and recon-
structed; below-
view of the
Cracow Gate

Very few Polish towns have been praised so much by Polish writers as Sandomierz on the Vistula where that river is joined by the San.

The town is beautiful. Its priceless oldest historic building is the former Dominican Church of St. James, built of brick in 1226. Art lovers will admire the Gothic Cathedral with unique and perfectly retained 15th-century frescoes in the Byzantine-Old Russian style. They recall the time when Sandomierz was a major trade centre at the crossing of roads to Ruthenia and Hungary. The Sandomierz townsfolk prospered and built fine houses. One of those houses belonged to the famous Polish 15th-century chronicler Jan Długosz. The town flourished in the Renaissance period, when the Town Hall with a fine parapet wall was built, as well as the Market Square houses. In Baroque times the Benedictine Convent, St. Paul's Church and a synagogue were added. Among curious objects are some bone chess pieces from the 11th century excavated by archaeologists. Among curious events, in 1843 a flood swept away several dozens ancient coffins from the cathedral vaults waiting outside for cremation and floated them down the river scaring local peasants to death. Among the legends, there is one saying that a mad bull once engraved the inscription *Salve Regina* with its horn on an ancient mound to make people more pious.

The old architecture of Sandomierz makes a wonderful sight on the high Vistula escarpment, with the river meandering at the foot of

the town between the edges of the Kielce-Sandomierz and the Lublin uplands. Pressed by its several swift Carpathian tributaries, the Vistula shifts its bed all the time. Watched from above, the numerous old river beds look like a whirling mass of snakes.

The village of Wrzawa at the marshy confluence of the Vistula and the San has a very bad reputation among the locals from the Sandomierz Forest. They imagine the area to be the gate to hell. The surrounding bogs, quagmires and wicker are crowded with kelpies, lamias, nymphs and other water spirits, while on drier land common devils roam. However, they are pretty hard to meet these days. Maybe they have been frightened off by TV and cars, or got intoxicated by sulphuric exhausts.

For, on the other bank of the Vistula almost exactly opposite Sandomierz, lies Tarnobrzeg, the centre of the sulphur industry existing for 40 years and bringing high profits to Poland from its exports.

The huge fortified Krzyżtopór castle at Ujazd was erected in the 17th century on a pentagonal plan by Italian architect Lorenzo Senes.

Built for the Ossoliński family, it was to sym-
bolize their power and glory, and most of all
their solidity. The number of castle towers
equals that of the seasons of the year; there are
as many halls as months, as many chambers as
weeks and as many windows as days in the
year. The designer's (or his employers') fantasy
went so far as to replace the ceiling of one chamber in the biggest tower with an aquarium full
of exotic fish. It is a great pity that this excellent
example of Mannerism was reduced to ruin after only a decade from its building, i.e. in 1655
during the Swedish 'Deluge'. Another reminder
of the Ossoliński family's generosity is the
church at Klimontów, also abounding in strange
and quite impractical solutions.

And so the picturesque River Vistula, en-
veloped in legends reaches the town of
Kazimierz Dolny - even more beautiful than
Sandomierz, if this is at all possible. It is here
that painters have been coming by the thousands for a century now to contemplate and
paint nature. Kazimierz is the town they love
most, next only to Cracow. The charming Renaissance and Baroque town spreading over sev-

*Nałęczów,
a cardiotherapeu-
tic spa. Baroque
palace in the
sanatorium park*

163

Kazimierz Dolny. Market square with a view of the Parish Church; Renaissance house of Przybyła

Końskowola. Interior of the Baroque Parish Church

eral hills and deep ravines has become Poland's, and especially Warsaw's, open-air salon. The well-maintained houses of rich burghers: the Przybyła (late-Renaissance), the Gdańsk (Baroque) and the Celej (Mannerist) houses have fine gables and richly ornamented façades. When sightseeing in Poland you can skip a lot of towns, but certainly not Kazimierz. Nearby on the right bank of the Vistula we find another attraction - Puławy. At the end of the 18th and the beginning of the 19th centuries this residence of the powerful Czartoryski family functioned as an extension of the capital. It was an impor-

*Puławy
on the Vistula.
Baroque palace
remodelled in the
neoclassical style,
surrounded by
an old park*

tant political, cultural and philosophical centre competing with Warsaw. While the modern trend of the Enlightenment reigned at the court of Stanisław Augustus Poniatowski, at Puławy they were in for sentimentalism. After the king's abdication the Czartoryski family were treated with such respect as if they were a substitute dynasty for the time of enslavement. They remodelled the former Baroque Lubomirski Palace into a neoclassical residence, surrounded by an unusually beautiful park with a romantic Temple of Sibyl encircled with Doric columns.

In the neighbouring spa town of Nałęczów, with mineral water rich in iron, two great writers, Bolesław Prus and Stefan Żeromski, liked to stay and strengthen their hearts. Żeromski, a dissident struggling against the Tsar, set up a clandestine political centre at Nałęczów camouflaged as some educational institutions and cooperatives. A majority of state leaders in the soon-to-be-independent Poland were instructed there.

At the opposite, south-eastern end of the Lublin region lies Zamość, which fully deserves its qualification as 'a pearl of the Renaissance'. Quite untypically, the town was designed and built on virgin land by the rich family of Jan Zamoyski, Chancellor and Grand Hetman of the

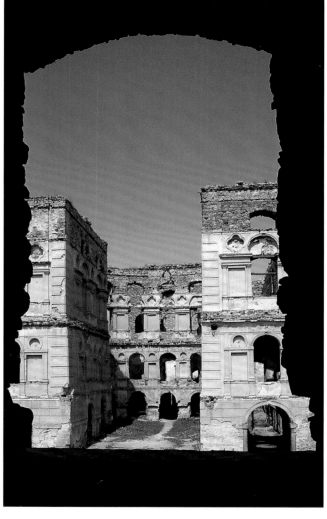

*Ujazd.
Ruins of the
Mannerist
Krzyżtopór
Castle*

165

Tarnobrzeg in the Sando-mierz Valley, a sulphur industry centre. Tarnowski Palace and Bartosz Głowacki Monument in the market square

Crown. He was the chief adviser to King Stephen Bathory, a Hungarian from Transylvania with a poor command of the language of the country he ruled. The king owed many of his successes to Jan Zamoyski, whose greatest merit was Zamość, designed and built by the Italian Bernardo Morando.

Having travelled around the whole region, let us now visit its main city. Lublin is very old; the first settlement dates to the 8th or 9th century. From the 12th century it served as a base for Polish eastward expansion into the Ruthenia. In return, it was often invaded by Lithuanians, Tartars and Ruthenians. The union of the Polish Kingdom and the Grand Duchy of Lithuania was signed in Lublin in 1569.

Sandomierz. Market square with the Renaissance Town Hall and old houses

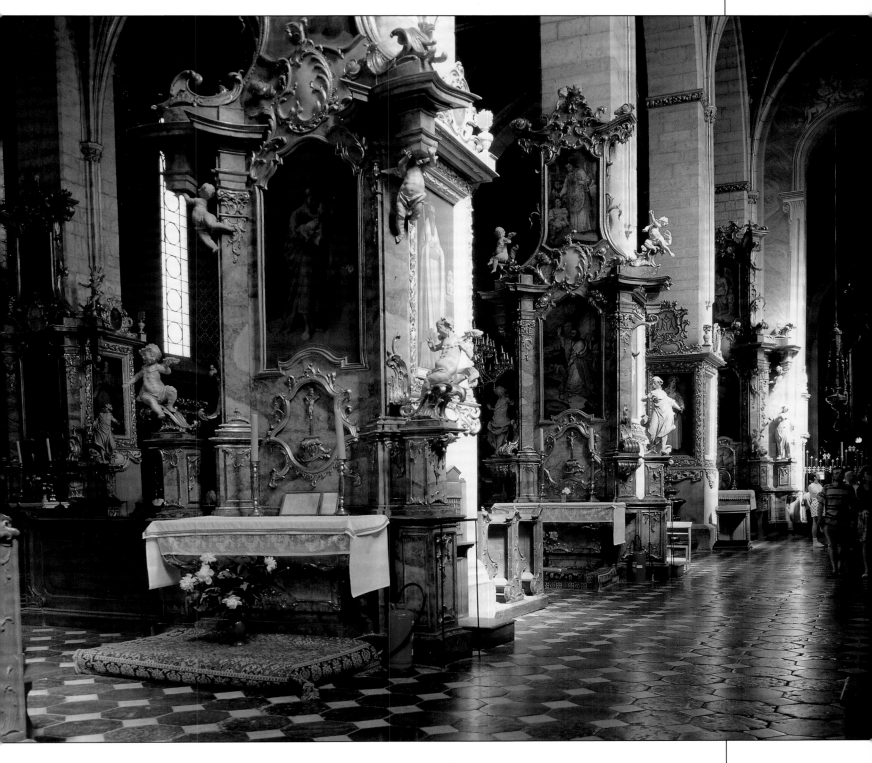

Of Lublin's numerous historic places, the Royal Castle is the most valuable. Its beginning dates back to the 14th century, but only the tower and Gothic Trinity Chapel have survived from that time. The Chapel contains a real treasure: the excellent Ruthenian-Byzantine murals founded by King Władysław Jagiełło in 1418. The city has a vast collection of churches in nearly every style met in the Polish lands - from Gothic to neoclassical.

At the end of 1944 and the beginning of 1945 Lublin was a temporary capital of Poland, where the Soviet-imposed Polish Committee of National Liberation resided. This sad fact is better forgotten.

Sandomierz, a town with beautiful architecture set in a fine landscape. Interior of the Cathedral of the Holy Virgin Mary

*Leżajsk
on the outskirts of
Sandomierz Forest.
Magnificent 17th-c.
organ in the
Bernardine
Church*

THE VESTIBULE
TO THE EAST

Przemyśl, a site of the earliest, palaeolithic settlement and an object of a centuries' long dispute between Poland and the Eastern Slavs. Fountain with a bear, the town's symbol; view of the town from the Tartar Mount and the 14th-c. castle extended in the 16th and 17th c.

*Sieniawa.
17th-c. Baroque
palace in a large
park*

In the south-eastern corner of Poland on the River San a beautiful town extends over seven hills like Rome. Przemyśl is a specific town, for it lies on the border of two civilizations: Roman and Byzantine. Since the dawn of its history, i.e. the 10th century, Przemyśl has been an object of Polish-

*Jarosław,
an old town with
nearly 2,000
years' history
extending over
the picturesque
hills on the River
San. Market
square with the
imposing,
originally
Renaissance
Town Hall*

Ruthenian conflicts. They still echo today as the disputes over some places of worship, to which both the Roman Catholic majority and the Greek Catholic minority claim their rights. The latter, mostly Ukrainians, recognize papal supremacy but have remained faithful to their eastern rite. Luckily, these epic quarrels do not spoil the steadily improving relations between Poland and its big neighbour, the Ukraine.

A magnificent view of the town extends from Castle Hill, where some fragments of the Renaissance castle built over much older, probably pre-Romanesque foundations have been preserved. Although the town is dominated by the Baroque style, it has a somewhat 'Eastern' atmosphere. The local museum boasts a splendid collection of icons, closely connected with the eastern rite. Przemyśl will be interesting for those who study the mingling of cultures and for military art lovers. The town, which used to be one of the strongest forts of modern Europe, fiercely contended over during the First World War, is still encircled by imposing 19th-century Austrian fortifications.

The environs are quite interesting. The village of Haczów in the Dynów Foothills is inhabited by Swedes, the descendants of Swedish soldiers taken prisoner in the 17th century. Although completely Polonized, they are still aware of their origins. Some areas are inhabited by Boyks and Lemks, a people close to Ukrainians. They cherish their traditions and (less and less often) their dialect.

Kalwaria Pacławska, the 18th-c. Franciscan monastic complex. Church interiors

Krasiczyn. Renaissance-Mannerist Krasicki Palace

*Dubiecko.
16th-c. palace
with the mu-
seum of poet
Ignacy Krasicki*

*Miejsce
Piastowe.
The Church of
Our Lady Queen
of Poland and
the Michaelite
Monastery*

*Lesko,
a tourist centre
of the Bieszczady
Mountains.
Jewish cemetery
with interesting
tombstones;
19th-c. Town
Hall*

Lake Solińskie, an artificial reservoir good for water sports and recreation

Solina. Dam on the San and a street for tourists

The region abounds in palatial ensembles. The Krasicki Castle at Krasiczyn, built by the Italian Appiani (the Poles in the past liked to employ Italian architects!), is one of the most precious examples of late Renaissance with some ornamental Mannerist details. The stately fortified early-Baroque castle of the Potocki, and earlier Lubomirski families at Łańcut houses a museum of carriages. Sieniawa has the residence of the Sieniawski, later Czartoryski families. Jarosław, which dates back to the times of King Bolesław Chrobry, offers quite an attraction: the vast, multilevel cellars and dungeons under the Old Town are open to visitors. The huge organ in the Bernardine Church at Leżajsk, set in the extremely opulent Baroque and Rococo interior, is said to match or even surpass that in Oliwa Cathedral. Sanok lacks great historic buildings, but its museum in the former Royal Castle owns the largest icon collection in Poland, the oldest of which come from the 14th century. The arcaded burghers' houses at Krosno date back to the 16th century and the tower of the late-Gothic Parish Church contains the second biggest bell in Poland next to the Zygmunt in Cracow - the Urban bell weighing 5 tons.

The countryside is rather poor. Most of the 19th-century Polish emigrants to the dreamland of America came from this region. The area underwent a short period of prosperity when oil was discovered here. The invention of the refining process and the construction of the first kerosene lamp by Polish engineer Ignacy Łukasiewicz at the village of Bóbrka instigated the worldwide career of the oil industry. And what progress - no more candles! Unfortunately, the Carpathian oil resources turned out to be small and they were used up quickly. Although some oil rigs still exist, they are monuments of technology rather than having any significant economic meaning. Of greater meaning are the mineral springs at Rymanów and Iwonicz, where the saline waters with high iodine and bromine content have strong medicinal properties.

More spas - Żegiestów, known for its waters with high iron content, Piwniczna, picturesque Rytro and Szczawnica - lie westwards in the vicinity of Nowy Sącz, in the past a market town on the route to Hungary, now an important centre of mountain tourism. The most famous of Polish health re-

Sanok. Jagiellońska Street in the town centre; Museum of Folk Architecture

Łańcut. 17th-c. Castle rebuilt in the French neo-Baroque style with the Carriage Museum in the former coach-house

Rzeszów on the River Wisłok, first settled in the neolithic period. Market square with the Town Hall remodelled in the 19th c.; the Baroque Lubomirski Palace

sorts (apart from Ciechocinek) is Krynica. Its mild climate and highly curative waters attract growing numbers of visitors. Some of them come for health, some for entertainment. In the period between the two world wars the world-famous Polish tenor Jan Kiepura used to come and stay in Krynica.

In the most distant tip of Poland, squeezed between Ukraine and Slovakia, the Bieszczady Mountains stretch wild and beautiful, forming the Bieszczady National Park. The least populated region of Poland, least interfered with by man's economic activity, has very few roads. The hills covered by deciduous and mixed forests and by vast meadows called *połoniny*, where grass is waist-high, tempt bold hikers, as do clean streams running through tunnels of greenery and the artificial Lake Soliński, perfectly fitting into the landscape. The land is ideal for tourists who look for pristine nature rather than luxury. They will find large areas of forest, meadows and bushes around the massifs of Tarnica, Halicz and Wielka Rawka, where it is easier to spot a bear's footprint than

Kolbuszowa. Ethnographic Park with the museum of regional building methods

Cmolas, a village developed from a forest settlement. Religious celebrations with a procession

Głogów Małopolski, the first settlement in Poland with a Renaissance town plan. Town Hall in the market square

then hired for a fat fee by other towns. No one else knew so well how to inflict long and cruel tortures to wrongdoers. Today some Biecz dwellers want to deny the 'black story' of their town, while others are proud of it, for in their view every field of activity demands the attaining of perfection.

Rzeszów, the capital of the region, has but a few historic relics. Worthy of seeing are the 19th-century pseudo-Gothic Town Hall and the monastery complexes of the Bernardine and Piarist monks, including the Regional Museum.

Biecz, a beautiful town on the hills. View of the late-Gothic Parish Church

Tarnów. Market square with the 15th-c. Town Hall rebuilt in the Renaissance style a century later

a man's. Some dozen bears live in the area and many more wolves. Quick-moving lynx and wild cat occur, to say nothing of deer and boar. Watch the ground carefully not to tread on a viper. A small number of non-venomous large Egyptian cobra live in the trees, the species completely extinct outside the Bieszczady region.

Whoever likes horror stories should pay a visit to the little town of Biecz, once called 'little Cracow'. Apart from a number of Gothic and Renaissance historic monuments and fragments of medieval fortifications, the somewhat grim attraction of the town's history was the school of public executioners, which trained masters in the craft,

Nowy Sącz in the Sądecka Basin. Eclectic Town Hall from the end of the 19th c. in the middle of an exspansive market square

FOR DESSERT – THE TATRAS

Chamois,
a curiosity of the
Tatra fauna

It is hard to believe that people in the past hated the mountains. In the Middle Ages they were considered unworthy of any attention, awful and dangerous, just standing in the way. In the early Renaissance mountains were in favour for a short while, admired by Dante and Petrarch. But the fascination was short-lasting. In the 16th century Montaigne called mountains (and seas) the most boring things in the world. Outstanding naturalist Buffon thought that 'nature in its primeval state is dead and repulsive'. Voltaire treated the Alps as an obstacle that divided nations.

The world has made progress, for most people today love mountains and regard them as the most wonderful phenomenon.

Shelter on Lake
Morskie Oko in
the High Tatras

The Poles, especially those who have never seen any other mountain ranges, claim that the Tatras are the most beautiful of all mountains. Foreign visitors are also ready to

The High Tatras are steep alpine mountains with countless precipices, lakes and streams. Mnich above Lake Morskie Oko

Zakopane, the most popular holiday resort in Poland since the 19th c. Krupówki, the main street of the town

Zakopane attracted many artists in the past with its unique atmosphere. Villa Atma, the museum of composer Karol Szymanowski; his portrait in pastel by Witkacy

admit that - the Alps being twice and the Himalayas four times as high - the Tatra scenery is really of comparable beauty.

But before we venture to the very brink of Poland, the Tatra summits, it is well worth making a detour to the east in order to visit the Pieniny Mountains. Two times lower than the Tatras, the miniature Pieniny are a real gem. At their foot runs the swift Dunajec, which offers a thrilling experience: a trip by raft over the rapids and cascades of its gorge.

The highest Pieniny massif, Trzy Korony (Three Crowns) is only 982 metres high, but it is extremely diversified in form, with barren walls, sheer drops of two hundred metres, jagged rocks and ravines. The most popular is the Homole ravine in the Little Pieniny, higher then the main ridge. The fauna and flora are unique, abounding in rare species untypical for other Polish mountains, with many endemic ones not occurring anywhere outside the Pieniny. They are protected by the national park, now threatened by the dammed water of the Dunajec, the project carried out despite strong protests and demonstrations by the ecologists and young supporters of the green movement.

On fine days, the majestic range of the Tatra Mountains, piercing the clouds with its sharp peaks, is visible from many distant localities of the Cracow region. The most splendid view of the Tatras is from the deep basin of Podhale, the region of highlanders, a proud people gifted with exuberant imagination and using their own dialect. They reveal enormous artistic talents. Their music and dances, architecture, wood-carving and sculpture, their leg-

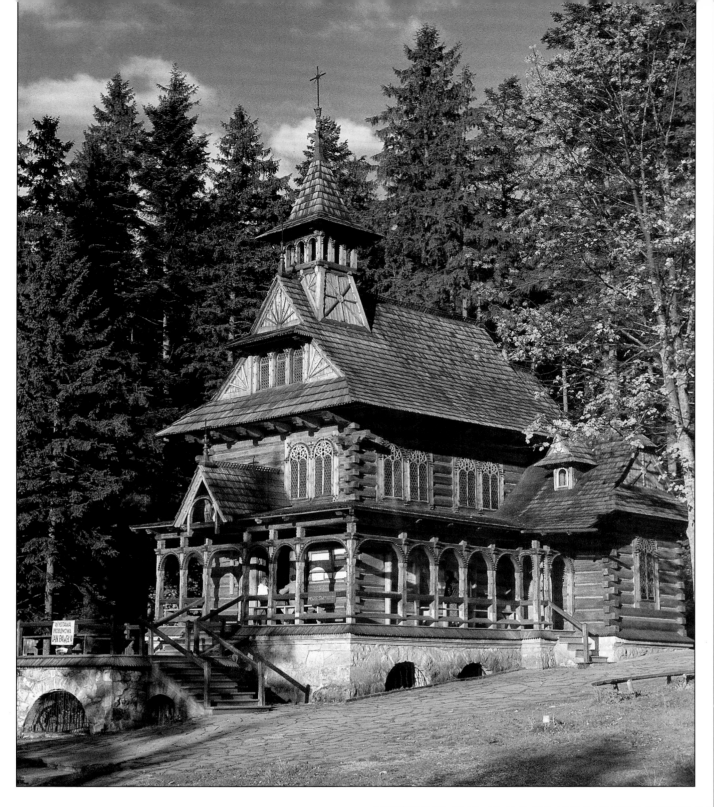

*Zakopane.
Chapel at
Jaszczurówka,
built in the
Zakopane style
conceived
by S. Witkiewicz*

*Cemetery of
famous personali-
ties in Zakopane*

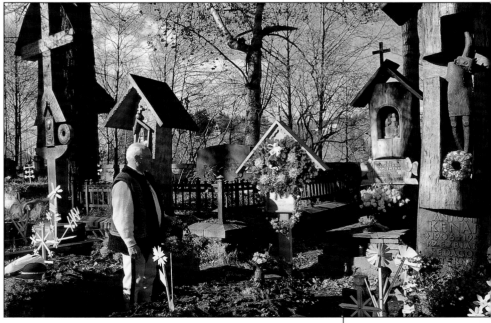

ends and funny folk tales are a jewel in Polish folklore. In the villages at the foot of the Tatras the highland traditions are sparkling with life. Here the colourful and ornate highlanders' costumes are worn not only on special occasions. The rich folk culture of the Podhale region bears many traces of influence from the neighbouring pastoral peoples, such as the Rumanian Valachians, Moldavians, Slovaks and Hungarians, as well as by settlers from historic Ruthenia and Germany, and numerous Gypsies.

The Tatras are the highest and the most diversified range of the long West Carpathian chain - young mountains almost untouched by erosion. The highest summits of the Tatras are Gerlachovka (2655 m) and Lomnicky (2632), both in Slovakia. Most of the Tatras lie outside Poland.

The Western Tatras. Kościeliska Valley

Carline flower, the inspiration for ornaments in the Podhale region

Some peaks lie on the Polish-Slovak border, like Rysy, the north-western top of which is the highest peak in Poland, and Kasprowy Wierch most important for skiers as the only peak accessible by cable car and two chair-lifts. In order to protect the tranquil environment for alpine animal species, such as chamois, marmot and bears, the Tatra National Park management categorically refuses permission to install any other skiing or tourist facilities.

Caves abound in the Western Tatras and are visited by potholers and tourists. Kasprowa Niżna Cave; Raptawicka Cave, open to visitors

Strict rules of environmental protection apply to the whole Tatras. Hopefully, they will not be moderated in spite of the skiers' unceasing protests. It is to these regulations that we owe fresh spring meadows carpeted with violet crocuses, crystalline water in lively mountain streams, and still a great deal of wild and inaccessible Tatra backwoods, where only the most experienced hikers can sometimes get. The magnificent Tatra lakes also have maintained their natural state and pure water. Lake Morskie

Crocuses proliferate in the spring meadows of the Chochołowska Valley

Podhale region – view towards the Tatras

Hang-gliders over the Tatra ridge

Oko (34.5 ha) at the foot of the sheer crags of Mięguszowieckie Turnie enchants everyone.

Giewont, towering over Zakopane, is a symbol of the town. An easy tourist trail ascends at the back of the mountain, but the difficult and dangerous north wall presents a constant challenge to amateur mountain climbers. Dozens of them have lost their life. Giewont is also a cult place, connected with the legend about the Sleeping Knights, similar to folk tales of many European countries. The knights from Giewont are a great puzzle, for the legend has

Highland folklore: a fine group of sledges and highlanders in traditional costumes

Bukowina Tatrzańska, a big highlanders' village. Interior of an old church

Zubrzyca Górna. Orawa (Orava) Ethnographic Park - interior of an Orawa hut

about a dozen versions, differing from one another on such issues as when they fell asleep and why, who put them to sleep and what for and when they are going to wake up. If we accept the prevailing view that when they wake up, they will free Poland from foreign rule, they should surely be by now awake.

The narrow Tatra valleys squeezed deep in the mountains are no less popular than the peaks. Year by year thousands of vacationers come to walk there and breathe some invigorating mountain air. Most of these valley promenades are situated in the Western Tatras, slightly lower and gentler than the High Tatras.

In the past, the Podhale region was full of highwaymen, not legendary at all. The highlanders' favourite hero, named Janosik, lived and robbed on the southern, Slovakian side of

Ząb near Zakopane. Colourful Corpus Christi procession

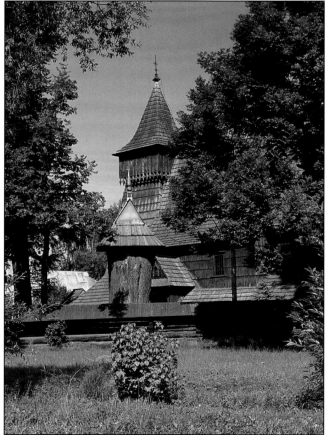

Dębno. 15th-c. wooden church of St. Michael the Archangel

the Tatras. He has been immortalized in countless songs, plays, novels, paintings and music pieces. Like Robin Hood, he robbed the rich and helped the poor. For his moral conduct he was caught and tried and sent to the gallows in 1713.

The lowlanders continue to cherish the myth of an old Zakopane, a wooden village at the mountain foot which at the beginning of the 20th century was so darling to the greatest Polish musicians, painters, writers, philosophers and politicians. Forty, maybe thirty years ago it still looked like that. Today it is a big town - not too beautiful, not very coherent and very crowded. No matter what, a trip to Zakopane is a must at least once a year. Not even the youngest generation would give up this tradition.

The Dunajec Gorge, a beautiful river canyon cutting through the Pieniny Mountains.
Raft trip

Niedzica. Fortified castle over the Dunajec Gorge connected with the legend of lost Incan treasure

Shrine –
a frequent sight
in the Podhale
region